Chelsea Brooke Yarborough

PROCLAMATION BEYOND THE PULPIT

The Expansive Homiletical Practice of Black Women

BAYLOR UNIVERSITY PRESS

Cover and book design by Elyxandra Encarnación
Cover images: (Nannie Helen Burroughs, *top right*) Miss Nannie Helen Burroughs, Schomburg Center for Research in Black Culture, Jean Blackwell Hutson Research and Reference Division, New York Public Library Digital Collections. (Sojourner Truth, *middle left*) Portrait of abolitionist Sojourner Truth, sitting with yarn and knitting needles, 1864, Schomburg Center for Research in Black Culture, Photographs and Prints Division, New York Public Library Digital Collections. (Fannie Lou Hamer, *bottom right*) Fannie Lou Hamer, Mississippi Freedom Democratic Party delegate, at the Democratic National Convention, Atlantic City, New Jersey, August/WKL, 1964, photograph by W. K. Leffler, retrieved from the Library of Congress.

Library of Congress Cataloging-in-Publication Data

Names: Brooke Yarborough, Chelsea, 1990– author http://id.loc.gov/authorities/names/n2025001001 http://id.loc.gov/rwo/agents/n2025001001
Title: Proclamation beyond the pulpit: the expansive homiletical practice of Black women / Chelsea Brooke Yarborough.
Other titles: That'll preach http://id.loc.gov/resources/hubs/05a41890-9252-fc99-7eaa-f9dcf843443d
Description: Waco, Texas : Baylor University Press, [2025] | Revision of the author's thesis (PhD, Vanderbilt University, 2021) under the title: "That'll preach" : decentering the pulpit through the non-pulpit homiletical practice of Black women. | Includes bibliographical references. | Summary: "Centers the preaching practices of Fannie Lou Hamer, Nannie Helen Burroughs, and Sojourner Truth to derive homiletical insights from these non-pulpit preachers"—Provided by publisher.
Identifiers: LCCN 2024059152 (print) | LCCN 2024059153 (ebook) | ISBN 9781481323024 paperback | ISBN 9781481324243 library binding | ISBN 9781481323048 adobe pdf | ISBN 9781481323031 epub
Subjects: LCSH: Truth, Sojourner, 1799–1883 http://id.loc.gov/rwo/agents/n79138780 | Burroughs, Nannie Helen, 1879–1961 http://id.loc.gov/rwo/agents/n92092977 | Hamer, Fannie Lou http://id.loc.gov/rwo/agents/n79151531 | African American preaching—History—19th century | African American preaching—History—20th century
Classification: LCC BV4221 .B76 2025 (print) | LCC BV4221 (ebook) | DDC 251.0082—dc23/eng/20250621
LC record available at https://lccn.loc.gov/2024059152
LC ebook record available at https://lccn.loc.gov/2024059153

"Yarborough offers us a vital text for the future(s) of homiletic discourse and practice. *Proclamation Beyond the Pulpit* challenges our assumptions about where and how people engage in religious meaning-making, even as it interrogates the very impulses behind these practices. These pages lay the groundwork for examining our moral resources, contexts, epistemologies, pragmatics, and embodied integrity—while unapologetically exploring the fugitive histories of Black women's sacred rhetoric. Taken seriously, this work disrupts the tidy categories within homiletic discourse that have never truly reflected the lived realities of religion on the ground. We've been gifted an urgent and long-overdue contribution to the resources that center religion, society, and the reimagining of collective accountability."

Lisa L. Thompson, Associate Professor and Cornelius Vanderbilt Chair in Black Homiletics and Liturgics, Vanderbilt University

"By helping us imagine the possibilities of preaching beyond the pulpit place, Yarborough helps us imagine the activity of the Holy Spirit in new ways. Of course, stories of African American women's knowledges are the vessels for what is new and necessary. This is a moment in the United States when we need the new, both ancient and untried. This timely text is for anyone—preacher, laity, artist, teacher, activist, prophet, healer, seer, or sage—who is about the business of creativity and justice."

Nancy Lynne Westfield, Director, Wabash Center for Teaching and Learning in Theology and Religion

"There is so much at stake in Chelsea Yarborough's description of Black women preachers. Centering the voices of Sojourner Truth, Nannie Helen Burroughs, and Fannie Lou Hamer to define preaching's purpose and method brings proclamation's life and death exigency into view. Often, books on preaching method are leveraged for gatekeeping. Yarborough leverages her astute methodological insights to throw wide preaching's gate to God's expansive Word. This book believes in preaching's power to change the world—pulpit or no."

Jerusha Matsen Neal, Associate Professor of Homiletics, Duke Divinity School

"In *Proclamation Beyond the Pulpit*, Chelsea Brooke Yarborough offers an essential contribution to the understudied practice of preaching outside traditional ecclesial environments. This well-researched, interdisciplinary book highlights the sacred rhetoric of three pioneering Black women: Sojourner Truth, Nannie Helen Burroughs, and Fannie Lou Hamer. Yarborough's work expands the potential figures that deserve inclusion in the history of preaching while also offering new methodologies and practices for the work of proclamation amid the urgent challenges of our time. I suspect that this illuminating text will have a lasting impact on the field of homiletics."

E. Trey Clark, Assistant Professor of Preaching and Spiritual Formation, Fuller Theological Seminary

This book is dedicated to Sojourner Truth, Nannie Helen Burroughs, Fannie Lou Hamer, and all Black women who preach regardless of permission or platform.

This work is from you and for you.

May you receive this love letter to your methodological brilliance and as gratitude for the gifts you have and continue to pour out.

CONTENTS

ACKNOWLEDGMENTS

I am grateful to live a life of co-creation, grounded in a fullness of community and communion with myself, God, and so many beautiful people that surround me. This journey was no different. Thank you all.

God, thank you for the ways your Spirit dances above, within me, and around me in unconditional love.

Sojourner Truth, Nannie Helen Burroughs, and Fannie Lou Hamer—thank you for your witness and homiletical methodology. We are better because you chose to proclaim and because of the power of your practice. I am better for having sat with you in this work. Thank you for drawing me near to myself because of the ways you stayed near to yourselves despite everything around. This work is possible because of you.

Janie, Jeannette, Helen, Dorothy, Inez, and Jean—I am me because of who you are and were. Thank you for being my teachers here and beyond. I am still listening.

To my family—Dan, Mom, Dad, and all the folks—thank you for foundations to learn and grow from. To my friends—I am here because you check on my being before my doing. Thank you for reminding me to be well amidst it all. To my teachers and mentors—thank you for your work, wisdom, care, accountability, push, and encouragement. Dale and Gail—thank you for still finding ways to show up. To my students—thank you for teaching me to always learn. To my writing group turned sisterhood—thank you for a space to create in community.

To my love and forever teammate in this life, RCNYG, thank you for a love that makes fear superfluous. You are honey for a weary throat. I learn so much from you. I love you always.

To each of you whose love lifts me, know that my gratitude extends beyond what I could muster in a few paragraphs. As much as I love words, they continue to fall short as I try to thank you all. I trust that you know who you are and feel the depth of my gratitude. I love you deep.

Finally, to each of you who picked up this book—thank you for exploring with me. May it encourage you, challenge you, and ask you to expand. May we proclaim justice, hope, and possibility in a world that needs it deeply. May we practice even more than we proclaim.

1
Introduction
That'll Preach: Black Women's Non-Pulpit Preaching

"Sis! That'll preach!" I turned my head to see an older Black woman yelling this from an appetizer-filled table at the local open mic night. I was eighteen, and this is the first time I remember someone yelling this to me from a crowd. I had heard the phrase before, but this time something resonated instead of repelled me from the thought that somehow *I* was preaching. This time this calling was directed to me, in a coffee shop, over poetry. I was struck, because preaching as I knew it and this scene didn't seem to line up. When I sat down, another Black woman found me and emphatically said, "You preached that thang right there." This time I responded with a laugh, "I'm not a preacher, but thank you!" She responded, "Says who?"

That'll preach. This phrase, commonly used in Black church traditions, signifies that something has impact and meaning for the hearer. I remember feeling excited that someone resonated with what I said but also hesitant because I never, ever thought myself to be a preacher. I had seen a few women preach in the pulpits of my childhood, but not many. Preaching and preacher were not even in my consideration for who I was and what I was doing. I saw too much evidence, reiterated by what people called "sacred" and "God's voice," that preachers were mostly men and preaching was always in a pulpit. However, while my head reasoned this, something else in me has always felt there was more to the story. God is simply too vast for God's voice and communication to be limited to one small space. Seven years after that open mic I preached my "initial sermon." I am clear now that this was my first time proclaiming in the pulpit, not my first time preaching. Preaching is a practice; and the pulpit is just one place where that practice occurs.

This is the seed that this work grows from. Its origins are autobiographical in many ways, and in turn it is relentless in its pursuit of the stories of other Black preaching women who have found expansive place for this proclaiming practice. This is a Black women centered homiletic, asking us to consider an expansive vision of preaching. I believe if we push ourselves to listen again widely, we too might find ourselves responding to new things with "That'll preach."

In this world where *Black* has signified *man* and *woman* has signified *white*, Black women have been understudied and underrecognized for their contributions across scholarly inquiry. Black women have not been seen as resources for theoretical inquiry, but theory has been ladened upon their works and their words. They have been theorized through an outsider gaze instead of theory being drawn directly from their practices, experiences, and theoretical assertions.

The field of homiletics has not escaped this trend in theory or practice. Black women have been lumped into scholarship as addendums and one-chapter insights within broader treatments of Black preaching and/or women's preaching. However, neither of these lanes alone has adequately considered the critical intersection of *Black* and *woman*. This intersectional identity requires an intentional look so that the genre of preaching is expanded beyond the confines of normativity. Without that engagement, there will always be gaps in understanding the work and preaching of Black women, and therefore the practice and possibilities of preaching at large.

Black women's preaching across diverse platforms and circumstances is critical to expanding our understanding of what preaching is and what preaching aims to do. The entangled relationship of preaching and the pulpit has created a limited scope for who can be considered a preacher. The pulpit has remained the primary locus and venue where we believe preaching occurs. Although Black women have historically proclaimed theology and Scripture in varied venues and spaces, these acts have not been called "preaching." However, when Black women's religious and sacred speech is brought to the forefront, regardless of where it is occurring, it expands the homiletic genre—and, more specifically, expands the scholarship beyond that which has previously aided the erasure of Black women's preaching practices. The aim of this book is to remove homiletical limitations of space and location, explore what Black women preachers throughout history teach us about preaching, and excavate the unique homiletical insights that emerge from these preachers.

This book first asks, What is preaching through the lens of Black women non-pulpit preachers? Specifically, what is preaching through the lens of the lives of Sojourner Truth, Nannie Helen Burroughs, and Fannie Lou Hamer? Underneath this inquiry are broader questions such as, What makes a moment of public proclamation "preaching" as opposed to simply a speech or another oratorical classification? What is the genre of "preaching" within the larger rhetorical category of public discourse? Preaching as a distinct genre of communication has evolved over time, yet in many ways it remains tied to institutional authority and/or the spatial demarcation of the pulpit. I believe that looking expansively at Black women's preaching challenges accepted definitions of preaching. Preaching as solely a pulpit practice misses the expansive *teloi* that are found when we examine preaching across platforms. Preaching as a political and subversive act occurs across institutional demarcations and within the greater realm of the world beyond the church.

I focus my study of Black women non-pulpit preachers on Sojourner Truth, Nannie Helen Burroughs, and Fannie Lou Hamer because they are all widely known for their work as activists and educators across different time periods. Although in some cases their rhetoric has been examined through the lens of political movements, they have not been explicitly studied as preachers—and more importantly, they have not been the source of homiletical insights. My intent is not to justify these women as preachers, but to invite their preaching voices, which operated in spheres beyond the institutional church and pulpit, to teach us about preaching in more capacious ways: Preaching as a political act. Preaching as activism. Preaching as a rhetorical response to the urgent needs of the world, with an urgent call for action at its core. Each of these preachers pushes us to see preaching in a new light and to develop the study of homiletics as a result.

This book adds a new framework to homiletics by centering the preaching of Black women non-pulpit preachers, who at best have been marginal but are mostly invisible in the conversation about preaching. This creates new windows to consider who is preaching and how change is ignited through the spoken word, as these women demonstrate. Studying them in this way does not enhance the field of homiletics alone. Opening their identity as preachers adds texture to their historical background and uncovers new questions about how their spirituality and sense of call from God and community was formative as they moved through multiple spheres. It offers new ideas regarding who they were and how they impacted the world around them. In addition, studying these women as preachers adds to their public witness as activists and educators, showing in more detail how they used their rhetorical prowess to shape the world around them. The intersection of being Black and a woman, along with the places that these women chose to inhabit, invites us to consider a new framework and new methodology for studying preaching, one that centers Black women in all of their particularity and exigency.

Here I propose a hermeneutic of intersectional particularity and exigency as a mode to study preaching. This is a critical intervention in the field of homiletics as it posits embodiment and particularity at the forefront of the rhetoric of a preacher. In this book I use biography as a foundational tool for understanding the rhetoric of these women. By starting with biographical information, I situate the women within their own stories and then investigate how they preached from those places of particularity, responding to the specific urgent exigencies impacting their communities. Without noting where they were, where they came from, and the exigent situations into which they spoke, we lose the depth and potency of their words and why and how they preached what they did. Sojourner Truth, Nannie Helen Burroughs, and Fannie Lou Hamer were all Black women non-pulpit preachers who aimed to create change. As such, biography gives us a lens into their embodiment in order to excavate the particular rhetorical situation they inhabited and created in their preaching. This hermeneutic of intersectional particularity and exigency serves as my methodological approach for understanding the preaching rhetoric of these women.

The Rhetorical Situation: An Intersectional Approach

A hermeneutic of intersectional particularity and exigency is a methodological approach that most simply means that the study of preaching cannot be detached from the preacher, their embodiment, and the concrete needs to which they were responding in the world. By adding this methodological layer to the study of preaching, I hope to texture how we engage preachers and how we listen for new understandings of preaching through a wider variety of proclaimers. Below, I turn to Lloyd Bitzer's "Rhetorical Situation" to support the idea that rhetoric is responsive to exigency, and, using Patricia Hill Collins and Sirma Bilge, I outline intersectionality as an analytical tool for critical praxis. I then posit that Sojourner Truth, Nannie Helen Burroughs, and Fannie Lou Hamer each enter their rhetorical situation with exigence at the forefront and from their experiences speak a word to humanity that is both specific to the moment and transcends their contexts. For these women, preaching was rooted in a demand for change, pushing against the systems around them for the purposes of a better life for Black women and the Black community at large. They believed their words might shift the outlook of their listeners beyond their immediate perspective and practice. From the depths of their unique embodiment in a particular place and time, these women were respondents to their situations, proclaiming hope in the inbreaking of a new world through God and the changed behavior of their hearers. This situates the discourse of Truth, Burroughs, and Hamer as urgent responses to significant personal, social, and historical exigencies, which offers nuance to the nature and purpose of preaching. As such, I frame my excavation of them through biography and a study of their rhetoric, because one without the other is an incomplete listening strategy for understanding their preaching.

The Urgency of Discourse

Preaching at best is responding to an exigence. It is a rhetorical situation spurred by the possibilities of change and forward movement in response to the good news expressed by the proclaimer. In "The Rhetorical Situation," Lloyd F. Bitzer argues, "An exigence which cannot be modified is not rhetorical; thus, whatever comes about by necessity and cannot be changed—death, winter, and some natural disasters for instance—are exigencies to be sure, but they are not rhetorical."[1] However, exigencies, urgent needs, and/or demands that are rooted in social injustice and aligned with the mishandling and abuse of particular people are indeed rhetorical because they can be changed. Truth, Burroughs, and Hamer were in many intransigent and oppressive institutions and systems. However, they knew that the social structures didn't have to remain in their current conditions, and they oriented their preaching as a response to the urgent situations around them.

When preaching occurs in the public arena, it is under the belief that the expressed discourse matters and is necessary for change. If an exigence can be modified by means other than discourse, it is not rhetorical.[2] This becomes especially true when preaching is responding to the demands of the external world, which can literally place the body of the proclaimer in harm's way.

This has been true for many Black women. If there was a way for change to occur without the use of such dangerous discourse, then certainly the preachers would choose it. The women at the center of this book engaged situations that required a discursive response. They believed that societal and communal change was not possible or would be as effective without rhetorical intervention. Their rhetoric was a necessary catalyst for action and movement beyond their current situation.

The proclaimer is not the only necessary party to consider in rhetorical discourse. The audience must be considered as well. Bitzer argues, "The 'rhetorical audience' must be capable of serving as mediator of the change which the discourse functions to produce."[3] Whether they seem capable or not, the possibility that the hearers of the discourse might be able to mediate change is a critical part of the rhetorical discourse. Truth, Hamer, and Burroughs's rhetoric was deeply contextual to their audiences. In order to invite change, their words needed to serve as a catalyst for change. Regardless of the audience's belief in their own capabilities or their willingness to change, they bore capacity to be part of the change proclaimed by these preaching women. The rhetorical situations created were situations in which responses to the exigencies presented were not only possible but invited.

However painful, unlikely, and difficult it was for Sojourner Truth, Nannie Helen Burroughs, and Fannie Lou Hamer to stand in front of their audiences, the exigence of their situations called forth their belief that their words mattered. They chose to speak when they could have chosen silence. They chose discourse in order to create a moment that required a response. They believed that change was possible even if the audience's response was to choose to ignore what they were saying. Bitzer continues, "In our real world . . . rhetorical exigencies abound; the world really invites change—change conceived and effected by human agents who quite properly address a mediating audience."[4] Change doesn't often come without a fight for those who are marginalized, disenfranchised, and abused by the society around them. That fight from Truth, Burroughs, and Hamer showed up in their practices and their preaching.

An Intersectional Approach

The rhetorical situation for Black women preachers is best understood through the lens of intersectionality. Bitzer offers a way to think about the dialectic between audience and proclaimer, and the urgency to which rhetoric responds. Expanding on this idea, it is crucial to prioritize the narratives of these women and their forms of embodiment. In order to better understand the rhetorical situations of these women preachers we must consider the intersections of power, identity, and social constraint that marked their courses of action. Without a clear consideration of their embodiment, we miss crucial elements from their stories that form the foundation of the meaning making in their words. In order to truly get at exigency and rhetorical situation, intersectionality from a praxis perspective becomes paramount.

Intersectionality as a term has taken on many different definitions.[5] For this book I lean on Collins and Bilge's definition:

> Intersectionality is a way of understanding and analyzing the complexity in the world, in people and in human experiences. . . . When it comes to social inequality, people's lives and the organization of power in a given society are better understood as being shaped not by a single axis of social division, be it race or gender or class, but by many axes that work together and influence each other.[6]

Intersectionality identifies an intention to see beyond one-dimensional readings of individuals and the communities in which they participate. It critically considers the systems of power that shape the lives of individuals and examines layers of privilege to get a fuller understanding of an individual's experience. As a tool, it supports our ability to see more robustly who people are and how who they are impacts their role and place in the societies in which they live. Putting intersectionality at the forefront also reminds us of the necessity of considering the myriad axes of power and privilege that impact a person's experience and the ways they are seen in the eyes of the society around them.

Within a perspective focusing on rhetorical praxis, intersectionality becomes an analytical tool for nuancing the rhetorical situation and engaging many intersecting elements of the narrative, embodiment, and identity of a proclaimer in order to glean insights from their *particularity*. In *Intersectionality*, Collins and Bilge expand the understanding of intersectionality as critical praxis, noting that when people think about intersectionality they often focus on either inquiry or praxis, but not the ways in which these two things intersect. Collins and Bilge argue,

> The praxis perspective does not separate scholarship from practice, with scholarship providing theories and framework, and practice relegated to people who apply these ideas in real-life settings or to real-life problems. Instead, this set of concerns sees both scholarship and practice as intimately linked and mutually informing each other, rejecting views that see theory as superior to practice.[7]

More pointedly, they note that by using intersectionality as an analytic tool, the theory of what is happening and how it is enacted are both present.

Intersectionality as critical praxis thickens the rhetorical situation for each of these preaching women by emphasizing the distinctness of the rhetoric of (and response to) their preaching. Their words are unique, deeply rooted in bodies and voices that rise from the nuances of their particular lives, which are lived at the intersection of many social and political forces. Exigent, intersectional preaching is about the development and practice of unique voices speaking to a world that needs it. Within the historical particularity of biography, under the framework of intersectionality, exigency serves as a tool to consider more deeply the sociological and political forces to which homiletical rhetoric is responding, which deepens and expands our ideas of the changes preaching mediates.

This method allows me to study Sojourner Truth, Nannie Helen Burroughs, and Fannie Lou Hamer beyond a one-dimensional reflection on their historical context—as actors on a historical stage. Even though they are all Black women occupying different moments in history, they were responding to different socioeconomic, gendered, and racialized situations. Intersectional thinking increases and enhances our sense of the different kinds of urgency into which these Black women non-pulpit preachers spoke, even as we consider meta-threads that are found throughout their preaching practices. Attending to their specific biographies, while noting both the differences and similarities that show up in their rhetoric, can teach us about the particularities of Black women's preaching across time while also further delineating the ways that the pulpit is an unnecessary prerequisite for the genre of preaching.

Intersectionality illuminates the complicated nature of identity and the ways that injustice preys upon particular identities and demographics. It also helps us consider the ways identities don't fit neatly into a box, and how a myriad of different things impacts each of us in different ways every day. The world is complicated, identity is complicated, and for Black women who move between multiple spaces, a complicated intersectional existence is normative. In this book, intersectionality is a tool to mark the specificity of identity within exigency as we engage the rhetoric of Sojourner Truth, Nannie Helen Burroughs, and Fannie Lou Hamer.

Each of the three women studied here are both Black and woman, yet beyond that their identities differ greatly, which is the gift of this book. I don't aim to flatten Black women's preaching into a neat paradigm of sameness; the gift of listening to rhetoric and learning from it is actually found in the particularity. By focusing my attention on Black women specifically, I am able to note the consistencies across these three particular women, as well as where they depart in their rhetoric. A layered analysis of their rhetoric not only provides space for new insight, but also suggests how the discipline of homiletics might be enhanced by the observations retrieved from this analysis.[8] Paramount is a multilayered analysis of the ways rhetoric is informed by the particularities of the whole self within a thickly understood context.

The Preaching Genre: An Overview of Black-, White Feminist-, and Black Women-Centered Preaching

To unpack the necessity of studying Black women non-pulpit preachers, I investigate the entangled relationship of the pulpit and preaching and discuss the limitations of studying homiletics solely as "pulpit speech." I ask, How does the privileging of the pulpit space and ignoring the critical intersection of *Black* and *woman* occlude Black women's inhabitation of the preaching moment in non-pulpit space? What do we miss in homiletics if Black women are not studied expansively, particularly given the limitations and exclusions of pulpit space? These questions are foundational as I consider what preaching is and who gets to decide. I survey foundational homiletic scholarship using three epistemological lenses to demonstrate how privileging pulpit space and not centering Black women's voices creates a hole in the scholarship. I aim to address that gap and build on this scholarship in this book through the study of the preaching practices of Sojourner Truth, Nannie Helen Burroughs, and Fannie Lou Hamer.

Black (Men) Preaching

The study of Black preaching is foundational for studying Black women non-pulpit preachers. Earlier scholarship on Black [men] preaching helped to move the academic understanding of the Black preacher beyond the sole focus on and description of a charismatic performance and into deeper analysis of performative nuances, theological underpinnings, and the communal telos of Black preaching. This scholarship makes clear that Black preaching cannot be subsumed into what might now be considered a "white homiletic." Any homiletic that doesn't specify its orientation and the sources of its data omits the necessary acknowledgment that we preach from our epistemological and experiential frameworks, and that that orientation matters. Black homiletic scholarship pushed that acknowledgment forward within the specific context of the Black church. As critical as this inquiry has been, it has still elevated two voices as the "standard" and/or normative mode of preaching: the preaching voice of men and preaching as a pulpit practice located predominantly in church spaces. It is important here to survey several key ideas and scholars in Black preaching to show their nuanced understandings of the nature and purpose of preaching, while also demonstrating the aforementioned limitations of male-centered pulpit preaching.[9]

Black preaching is a critical subject for scholarly inquiry but was not always deemed important as a source for intellectual study. *Black Preaching: The Recovery of a Powerful Art* by Henry Mitchell was the first of its kind, unveiling what it meant to be a Black preacher and why it mattered. In this book Mitchell offers an important history and analysis of Black preaching. He notes the significance of Black preaching as a form of orality in the lives of Black people that has served as an active part of their survival. Mitchell argues that Black preaching has "kept its believers alive and coping—even when in an oppressed condition that would have crushed many."[10] The sermon, then, is a dialogue between preacher and listener that stems from the preparatory work of God and preacher. This is carried out with the help of the Spirit, alongside the necessary work of the preacher and the congregation in the moment. His major contribution was illuminating the study of Black preaching as a viable subject for scholarly inquiry while demonstrating the importance of a Black homiletician writing about its nuances, its impact, and the roots of the ongoing practice—which primarily reflected the experience of Black male pulpit preachers.

Another foundational work on Black preaching is *The Heart of Black Preaching* by Cleophus LaRue. Expanding on Mitchell's work, specifically the hermeneutical approach to Black preaching, LaRue argues,

> In summary, powerful black preaching has at its center a biblical hermeneutic that views God as a powerful sovereign acting mightily on behalf of dispossessed and marginalized people. A belief in this God, an awareness of the sociocultural context of the black experience, and the creation of a

> sermon that speaks in a relevant and practical manner to the common domains of experience in black life, when taken together, ultimately result in a powerful sermon that resonates in a potent and meaningful way with those in the listening congregation.[11]

Black preaching has to connect to the experiences of Black life. Without that context, Black preaching loses the core of its identity and purpose, and the God proclaimed becomes misconstrued. Adding to Mitchell's argument, LaRue posits a specific theological orientation and a particular hermeneutic employed by the Black preacher. He identifies five domains of experience, or what he names as "tangible, corporeal situations in which the sovereign God's power is sought and demonstrated in the life experiences of blacks."[12] These domains are: personal piety, care of the soul, social justice, corporate concerns, and maintenance of the institutional church. The idea that our interpretive lens and our understanding of what constitutes Black preaching is rooted in cultural specificity is the most crucial addition of his work. Although he names some women when discussing the theology of preaching, LaRue's work is male centered and positioned explicitly within the context of the institutional church.

Celebration is a foundational practice in Black preaching that deserves critical engagement. In *They Like to Never Quit Praisin' God*, Frank Thomas posits that celebration is the orientation of the Black preacher because of the need to provide hope to listeners who live in a world that marginalizes and oppresses them. Celebration in worship is a subversive act within a society and world that often makes celebration feel impossible for Black people. Celebration is frequently signified by a particular expression that some call "whooping," which is followed by a response of shouting from the congregants and/or listeners. This aspect of Black preaching is critical, because without an intentional consideration of the content, purpose, and diversity of delivery found under the "celebration" umbrella, whooping can be caricatured as mere performance and delivery, especially from an outsider gaze.

Celebration is central to Black preaching, both in and beyond the pulpit, because it creates a space for hope and "next" in spaces where they could easily be ignored. However, celebration beyond the pulpit may render different responses than that from preaching within the context of worship.

Celebration doesn't exist without its counterpart, lament. Luke Powery writes, "The juxtaposition and unity of lament and celebration in preaching may be called a doxology because as a unified tensive pairing these manifestations of the Spirit in preaching represent the full glorification of God during times of joy and sorrow."[13] The relationship of celebration and lament reminds us that Black preaching at its best attends to the fullness of human experience and sees God in all of it. Lament is especially important as we consider Black women non-pulpit preachers and the particular exigencies they are responding to. The tension between hope and lament is present in their preaching as they take on systems that are actively aimed at their demise, while believing another world is possible.

Adding to this list of essential qualities of Black preaching, Kenyatta Gilbert argues in *The Journey and Promise of African American Preaching* that African American preaching is trivocal preaching.[14] The trivocal paradigm of the prophet, the priest, and the sage are critical elements that must be woven together within the preaching moment to accomplish what Gilbert posits *is* African American preaching. The prophetic voice speaks to "God's justice and what God intends,"[15] which is dependent upon the relentless hope that this is not the end of the situation. The priestly voice focuses on the community at hand and cares for the congregation of hearers. Meanwhile, "the sagely voice interprets the congregation's historical and cultural legacy, namely its archival materials, and seeks to decode the complex signs, symbols and texts of a congregation's worship life."[16] This voice requires a preacher who stands with the people, not only in front of them. Gilbert's contribution of trivocal preaching to the understanding of African American preaching is significant because it organizes a typology for both the content of African American preaching and what it aims to do. This also counters the popular notion that the prophetic and the pastoral do not sit in the same spaces; Gilbert argues instead that it is paramount that the prophet, the priest, and the sage are all able to come forth through the voice of the preacher. While Gilbert focuses on the pulpit as the locus of preaching, this framework is portable. It can span beyond the pulpit, and its different components are potentially meaningful within a broader context of preaching.

This sampling of works on Black preaching written by Black and male-identifying persons highlights important things that are often centered in Black preaching. However, these scholars have struggled to include the voices of Black women at the same level as they do their Black male counterparts. Black women's voices have been subsumed into these frameworks as if gender identity weren't an essential component to consider. The arguments lifted through these works are true in Black preaching, yet they are not *all* that is true. Black preaching does not *only* occur within the four walls of the institutional church or in formal pulpits. This is even harder to recognize when the voices that have been prioritized are those that have had access to these spaces within the institution of the Black church. Through the study of Black women non-pulpit preachers, I aim to shift the center of the scholarship on Black preaching beyond the institutional pulpit practices of male preachers.

W(hite)omen PreacHers

Feminist methodologies and hermeneutics for preaching have put women at the center of their inquiries, which necessarily has moved the conversation about preaching away from the male-dominated sphere. In many feminist considerations of preaching, however, the critical identity marker of race is overlooked or dealt with as an accent rather than as the central conversation. Black women have been footnotes and/or mentions in the works of white feminist homileticians, without a deep dive into what Black women uniquely contribute and offer to preaching. Even with their shortfalls, white feminist ways of talking about preaching have expanded the conversation and created more entry points into what preaching is and how it can be done in ways that create more inclusivity. Feminist homileticians tend to resist hierarchical, traditional, male models of preaching and lean into a homiletic that is centered more *within* and *from* a community than above it or on its periphery.

Community is a priority in feminist approaches to preaching. In *Weaving the Sermon: Preaching in a Feminist Perspective*, Christine Smith asserts that "the content of preaching from a feminist perspective needs to reflect a vision of wholeness, a tapestry of human complexity and diversity. The prophetic edge of this kind of preaching calls the Christian community to integrative, weaving action in the world."[17] With an in-depth look at feminist preaching through theological, psychological, and other lenses, Smith offers a needed perspective that counters the normative homiletic that she is aiming to subvert. Her conversation around "remembering" as a feminist practice is especially important for understanding her contribution.

Smith makes clear that feminist preaching lifts the community and aims to center those voices that may have been forgotten in times past. This shift toward remembering our stories as a faithful practice and interrogating marginalized voices in homiletics implicitly invites work such as this one, which involves the elevation of the voices of Black women non-pulpit preachers.

Remembering is an important practice in feminist preaching, especially as it pairs with responding to the immediacy of the community in front of the preacher. Lucy Rose posits a model for communal preaching in *Sharing the Word: Preaching in the Roundtable Church*. Rose argues for preaching to be an act that collaborates with hearers, both in preparation and during the preaching moment. She asserts that holding authority as a preacher removes the interpretive onus from the community.[18] Instead, she proposes, "the preacher is simply the one responsible for putting the text and sermon as one interpretation into the midst of the community for the particular service of worship."[19] Deep listening and presence *with* hearers, as opposed to authority *over* them, are necessary for a homiletic that is relevant to the community and shaped by the needs of the community. This model of preaching invites the preacher to take a different type of authority (or, Rose might argue, to intentionally "lose" authority altogether), such that the hearers are participants in the proclaiming of the text. The conversation about authority and its uses is critical to feminist preaching. It also invites us to consider who has the luxury of "losing" authority in community, which highlights the lack of intersectionality present in this work. For the Black women non-pulpit preachers I engaged, participating in community wasn't about losing authority but asserting *communal* authority in ways that were deeply situated in the vocational, social, and political exigencies faced by a particular marginalized community.

Following this same trajectory of recovering women's voices and interweaving voices from the community, Mary Turner and Mary Lin Hudson name the violence done to people when they are silenced and aim to recover women's voices from this silencing in *Saved from Silence: Finding Women's Voice in Preaching*. Hudson and Turner argue that when someone is silenced it is an erasure of their identity, and they demonstrate how women are and have been silenced both in the church and the society at large. In their constructive work on how to recover silenced voices, Turner and Hudson assert that sharing narratives is paramount. They write, "Telling their stories has always been a way for women to authorize their own reality. As we listen to each other's stories, we begin to make sense of our own."[20] Their argument reminds us of the necessity of listening to and uncovering the voices that haven't been heard, both historically and in our contemporary context. They also name preaching as a subversive act for women because they are choosing and working to speak in a culture in which they are often silenced.

Metaphors for preaching that are more inclusive of the space women inhabited when excluded from the pulpit are important to feminist approaches. In *Preaching as Testimony*, Anna Carter Florence argues, "The story of Christian preaching is not just about the church's speech. It is also about the church's struggle, and the preacher's struggle, to come to speech: hearing it, naming it, attempting it, embodying it."[21] She argues for a recovery of the "testimony" preaching tradition and offers three stories of testimony as case studies: Anne Marbury Hutchinson (1591–1643), Sarah Osborn (1714–96), and Jarena Lee (1783–?). She makes clear that the tradition of testimony does not solely involve women, but when recovered it can show us women's preaching from their locations on the margins. Florence contributes an argument of the testimony preaching tradition that illuminates an embodiment of what we preach, not simply the words. Although the women she looked at were preachers under the normative understanding, testimony preaching spans beyond the pulpit because it encompasses the personal responses of proclaimers to the gospel, which are not confined to one space.[22] Testimony is not limited to a particular power structure, but stems from whatever truths are being ignited within the proclaimer and to which they bear witness. This understanding of preaching moves beyond a hierarchical order of institutional affirmations and places preaching in the voice of anyone with the unction to testify.

Aiming to continue to recover voices that had yet to be studied, Beverly Zink-Sawyer looks at Antoinette Brown Blackwell, Olympia Brown, and Anna Howard Shaw, three white preaching women of the nineteenth century who were ordained and formally affirmed as clergy but saw their ministry in the woman's suffrage movement. In *From Preachers to Suffragists: Woman's Rights and Religious Conviction in the Lives of Three Nineteenth-Century American Clergywomen*, Zink-Sawyer notes the ways that their convictions as pulpit preachers and their struggles as women in ministry prompted their transition from solely speaking in pulpits to moving into other spaces of the movement.[23] These women used the pulpit as a springboard to a more expansive call outside of the church. By excavating how their journeys from the pulpit supported their continued sense of call in other movement spaces, Zink-Sawyer, through the witness of Blackwell, Brown, and Shaw, creates a link between preaching within the church and preaching beyond the church.

Feminist preaching scholarship contributes to a reassessment of a normative, male-dominated homiletic. These scholars do the critical work of what we might call "a re-gendering" of this male-dominated and historically formally constructed pulpit practice by showing women's ways of preaching and pushing for new homiletical practices from these ways.[24] They challenge homiletics by utilizing liberation and feminist methodologies and offering hermeneutical and rhetorical strategies for preaching that aim to include the whole community, especially those who have often been marginalized. However, with the exception of the work of Beverly Zink-Sawyer, there is still clear prioritizing of church buildings and pulpits as a locus where the spoken act is occurring. In addition, feminist scholarship in preaching has come up short in addressing other identity markers and experiences that women bring to preaching. The important differences that Black women preachers contribute have been subsumed under the larger umbrella of "feminist" preaching. This type of whitewashing, which blurs women's identities, made it necessary for Black women scholars to center Black women's experiences and point out the importance of the embodied intersection of both *Black* and *woman* as something necessary to study.

Black Women Pulpit Preachers

Black women homileticians, alongside rhetoricians, theologians, and others, have created scholarship that attends to the necessary intersection of both *Black* and *woman*, alongside the other identity markers that Black women hold. This important scholarship that centers Black women has created a space where Black doesn't mean only male, and woman doesn't mean only white. Black women preachers have a space they can call their ideological home and not feel the need to contort their being into scholarship created by and for others. However, Black women homileticians have still generally prioritized the pulpit, and therefore Black women's preaching is still limited to a place that remains largely dominated by men.

Black women homileticians focus on what it means to be Black, woman, and a preacher. In *Weary Throats and New Songs*, Teresa Fry Brown uses an ethnographic approach to consider a homiletic through the eyes of Black women. Through narratives of call, growth, and spiritual practices, Fry Brown weaves a story about contemporary Black women preachers. She gives them space to testify to their experiences, illuminating both the beauty and the difficulty of being Black women and preachers, across different ages, denominational backgrounds, and regional differences. The Black church has not turned a critically reflective lens towards itself in regard to discrimination against and oppression of women as frequently as it has attended to conversations about race. Black women preachers have had to fight for space to be heard in the role of preacher in the church. Fry Brown argues, "Like their foremothers, many contemporary black women have creatively moved beyond the 'Big Chair Syndrome.' Many know that all ground is holy. God is everywhere. The tremendous power of the pulpit in the black church tradition can be liberating or oppressive."[25] Although Fry Brown's study deals with ministry as a church practice and preaching as a pulpit practice, her statement asserts that there are creative ways that Black women move beyond formal spaces and still have preaching ministries.

Another approach to studying Black women preachers has been to imagine criteria that constitute Black women's preaching, or what some scholars explicitly name "womanist" preaching. In *Toward a Womanist Homiletic*, Donna Allen builds on Katie Cannon's work to create a more specific set of criteria for what constitutes womanist preaching.[26] Allen adds to Cannon's list of criteria, which include but are not limited to: a focus on Jesus's life and humanity and not his gender, special attention to the way we talk about sexuality in non-oppressive ways, and continually expanding the ways we talk about God.[27] She writes, "In a womanist homiletic, the preaching event includes a dialogue about the rhetoric of the sermon where not only is linguistic violence exposed, but from this dialogue the theo-ethical praxis and language of the faith community is shaped."[28] In this, she is arguing that womanist preaching creates a new kind of language that is "emancipatory praxis," which subverts the system that uses language violent towards Black women and anyone else.

In the field of communication, Kimberly Johnson builds on these criteria through the lens of rhetoric. She notes that rhetoric as a field has done a poor job of highlighting Black women's sacred speech. In *The Womanist Preacher*, she focuses on contemporary preachers Claudette Copeland, Melva Sampson, Gina Stewart, and Cheryl Kirk-Duggan. She uses Stacey Floyd-Thomas's four tenets of womanism, which emerge from the four-part definition of womanism given by Alice Walker. Johnson ends the book with a list of twenty-two characteristics for womanist preaching, many of which reiterate the criteria presented by Katie Cannon and Donna Allen. These criteria are important because these Black women scholars are pulling from the experiences of Black women and from rhetoric that contributes to their flourishing.

When centered, Black women's stories as well as their practices lead us to the necessary particularities of sacred speech and preaching from their perspective. In *Ingenuity: Preaching as an Outsider*, Lisa Thompson rethinks preaching through the perspective of Black women. Thompson invites the reader to witness and learn from their preaching practice, arguing that centering Black women means that preaching must expand beyond a white and male-dominated homiletic. She is attentive to the lived and embodied experiences of Black women and the ways experience shapes their preaching practices. She argues that Black women's preaching has been marginal or even seen as deficient because it does not align with whiteness and maleness, which has been the dominant story: "Our imaginings have been overwhelmingly stifled by a default imagery of maleness and what masculinity looks like alongside whiteness; and in turn, anything that moves in contradiction to such imaginings is inherently deficient."[29] However, Black women are able to expand familiar practices into new spaces. In her discussion of celebration, frequently a staple in the conversation on Black preaching,

Thompson argues, "As celebration is engaged by Black women it may possess some communally expected content. . . . However, the use of the feminine and its appearance alongside and in combination with more expected content in both obvious and subtle ways is the most explicit form of ingenuity."[30] The familiar is tied with a more explicitly feminine identity, such that women's experience is a legitimate space to proclaim alongside the lived experiences of the community as a whole. *Ingenuity* gives the reader room to see the unique proclaiming practices of Black women and to consider how these practices are used beyond the pulpit as well.

Placing the narratives of Black women at the center of homiletics is necessary and sacred work. Instead of Black women being an addendum, these scholars center and learn from their preaching prowess and posit new ways of thinking about preaching through the practices observed. In addition to these scholars, anthologies of Black women's sermons have given more access to the rhetoric and diversity found in Black women's proclamation. Though this work is paramount for beginning the conversation about Black women's homiletical practice, it still privileges the pulpit and the institutional church. In doing so, we miss the possible expansion that arises from proclaimers whose voices were not found inside of churches, but at protests, in educational spaces, on platforms for civil rights, and in the streets. However, when we begin at the margins—as these scholars have done with Black women—we illuminate other aspects that must be explored and other identities that have been pushed to the periphery of our disciplines, if included at all.

The Limitations of the Pulpit

This book is rooted in the assertion that the pulpit is a limited space to study preaching, especially for groups of people like Black women for whom access to formal and institutionalized spaces of preaching has been severely limited. The exclusionary nature of such a space invites us to consider that preaching must not be held to such a small spatial boundary. The pulpit produces unsettling demarcations of power and is an inherently gendered space. This doesn't mean it cannot be an important place for proclamation;

however, it does mean the pulpit cannot be the only place preaching is studied.[31] As a result, this book explicitly moves beyond that space to consider other platforms in which Black women's preaching occurs.

The aesthetic of power as articulated through a focus on pulpit practice has limited how we think about the expansive nature of preaching. In *Sacred Power, Sacred Space*, Jeanne Halgren Kilde walks through the history of Christian worship by way of architecture and its evolution. Kilde addresses three types of power that show up in the worship space: divine power and/or supernatural power, social power, and personal power. In her excavation of how different facets of power intersect and are created in the worship space, she shows the development of the pulpit in relationship to these power dynamics. Referring to the work of J. Z. Smith, Kilde writes, "The distinctive ways in which religious sites organize or arrange the people who use them constitute an important component of the perceived holiness of a space."[32] In this vein, the organization of space deemed "sacred" offers an aesthetic proclamation about who is allowed to speak, who is important, and who is "less than" in the space—a pattern going back to biblical days. Even before the specificity of the pulpit within the church, the demarcation of sacred space within the walls and secular space outside of the walls already created a distinction from which contemporary preaching is built.

In the late second century and early third century CE, the first gatherings of the Christian church began to change. Instead of meeting over meals and in homes, other spaces were starting to signify "church." In these changes, a "bema" was formed. The bema was a platform built for clergy, and the rest of the room was for the worshippers. Kilde argues,

> The bema and the separation it created between the clergy and the ordinary worshippers indicate that Christianity was becoming increasingly institutionalized. The new clergy, presiding over the symbolic Eucharist services that were becoming the centerpiece of Christian worship, played a

> very powerful role, in effect mediating between the gathered assembly and the God they worshipped.[33]

Kilde shows us that the perceived power and authority of the bema, which later developed into the pulpit, was constructed as a result of institutionalization. This truth has carried into contemporary churches, where the pulpit signifies personal power used in the language of "call," social power that marks those who stand in it as set apart and/or more important, and divine power as it designates the venue through which God speaks. This ancient reality has contemporary consequences, as it has shaped who is deemed a vehicle for God's voice and who is not. In that same vein, we are made aware of who is preaching versus who is not by where we look for the oratorical authority that designates how God is shaping and moving in the world. While there are certainly nuances across different denominations and generations of church architecture, what has remained consistent is the set-apart place for the clergy to speak that is a signifier of power. The voice of God becomes rooted inside the church, via the proclaimer, from this specific location.

In addition to the power dynamics created spatially in the pulpit, the pulpit itself is rooted in a history of gender exclusion. In *The Gendered Pulpit*, Roxanne Mountford names problematic ways preaching is studied, specifically the lack of attention towards the reality that it is geared towards what she refers to as "the male body."[34] Studying actual embodiment in rhetorical performance is critical to making a full review of the nature and purpose of the rhetoric. Mountford argues, "Texts that were once a robust rhetorical performance have too often been reduced to texts studied without reference to their performative nature."[35] Without an attentiveness to the ways that the art of preaching has been signified by "manliness," we miss the nature of the gendered pulpit, how women preach, and what women add to the overall identity of the rhetorical genre of preaching.

Kilde and Mountford's arguments display the hierarchical nature of pulpit space, both aesthetically within the worship environment and ideologically as a male-dominated sphere. Preaching, then, becomes a pulpit art that women have to fight their way into because of the significations of its maleness. Black women pulpit preachers have faced pushback and marginalization from within their Black church context, alongside the marginalization and oppression from society as a whole. Many scholars note that the African cultures from which many early Black Americans came did not participate in such gender inferiority. However, as Black clergy reproduced white American clergy structures, the issue of "gatekeeping" pulpit preaching to exclude Black women was clear.[36] The preacher was male.

When you truly center women's voices, specifically Black women, the pulpit is not the only place for preaching or even a primary place to be considered. In this book, I consider preaching outside of the gendered pulpit. I wonder about new places of sacred demarcation and assess how an expansion of what we deem "sacred" might contribute to the growth and development of the art of preaching. Instead of acquiescing to an ideology that has asked women to "know their place" when outside of the pulpit, I highlight Black women who created new spaces of power and disrupted power centers through their preaching practices. They preached in expanded spheres that impacted the world in ways that were different, but in no way secondary, to preaching in the pulpit.

The following sections look at scholarship that has pushed the margins of the preaching genre beyond the pulpit in different ways.

Preaching: An Expansive Practice

The Four Codes Framing

Even as it is expansive, preaching as a genre of communication has threads of continuity across platforms. *The Four Codes of Preaching* is a helpful tool for examining the rhetorical function and purpose of preaching. In *The Four Codes*, John McClure creates a coding system that can be used to consider the ways in which homiletical speech is unique and what makes up this particular genre of sacred orality. I consider this system a bank of possibilities rather than an exhaustive coding system, as I wonder if there are other codes or ways of understanding the codes that could be added. However, genre studies allow us to identify what might mark preaching as preaching by engaging codes within the genre of preaching and noting when those codes change to another genre. McClure's system offers a framework for thinking about the genre of preaching, which serves my book well because the codes are a conversation partner for the insights gleaned from the Black women non-pulpit preachers I engage. One can use the four codes to push the assumptions of the preaching genre by engaging homiletical artifacts that are situated beyond normative understandings of preaching.

The four codes of preaching are the scriptural code, the semantic code, the theosymbolic code, and the cultural code. These four codes, in no particular order, create the patterns of rhetoric that McClure argues form the basis of homiletical artifacts. Each of the codes has an intertext: "a text lurking inside another, shaping meanings, whether the author is conscious of this or not."[37] Through the intertext, we see the code and the way meaning is being made within it. The four codes operate together and are informed by one another throughout the sermon. They aren't set out in a linear pattern but within the sermon are woven into one another almost like a rhetorical quilt that, together, constitutes the sermonic genre.

The scriptural code refers to "any direct or indirect verbal allusion of the biblical text or to the events to which the biblical text testifies."[38] The intertext for this code is *anamnesis* or remembering. McClure argues that all sermons move through this type of remembering to recall in some way, shape, or form the foundations of Christian faith. This remembering locates the sermon within a larger trajectory of the Christian tradition and refers back to truths considered through the stories and truths of the biblical text.[39] Without this referential point, the foundation of the sermon as connected to a larger history and tradition gets lost.

The semantic code looks at the message woven throughout the moves of the sermon. This code focuses on the words that the preacher chooses and what those words, phrases, and sentences then signify as meaningful. The intertext for the semantic code is truth: "Ideas in the sermon acknowledge the existence of truth, promote a certain kind of truth, and respond to certain expectations of truth."[40] McClure notes that this code is closely related to the scriptural code, in that truth in a sermon is often mediated through how one interprets and understands the biblical story, however loosely or broadly one thinks about it.

The third code is the theosymbolic code, and its intertext is worldview. The way that the preacher constructs this code produces a particular worldview that is aligned with that of the hearers, while often pushing against that worldview, as well, to make new meaning.[41] As McClure posits, "It is the preacher's own synthetic theological product."[42] Conceived narratively, McClure names giver, receiver, object, subject, helper, and opponent as six essential characters or actors in the sermon. These roles are ordered into particular ways based upon the preacher's viewpoint and offer the hearers a larger narrative to consider.

The final code is the cultural code, which looks at the way that the preacher utilizes the cultural norms of the listener such that the message is relevant and rooted in an actual context. This code refers to "every reference within a sermon to the broader culture in which the congregation lives its daily life."[43] Therefore, the intertext is experience. This code is what allows the sermon to sit inside a particular community and/or within a particular culture because of the use of references that the audience would understand.

Each of these codes offers a different look into the rhetorical strategy of the preacher. In most cases, this coding system has been used to engage pulpit preaching, outlining the myriad ways the rhetoric of sermons is formed. However, the broad nature of the coding system makes considerable room for preaching to be considered rhetorically without the bounds of tradition and/or institutional affirmation of the definition of preaching and preacher.[44] It invites consideration of works that fall within the codes but outside the pulpit. Again, this tool is a useful interlocutor as I listen to the sermons of Black women who were not known as preachers because they proclaimed outside of the pulpit.[45]

Beyond Rhetoric: The Quilted Sermon

Black women non-pulpit preachers are not only found in aural communication. In "Quilting the Sermon: Homiletical Insights from Harriet Powers," Donyelle McCray offers a new lens for preaching by positioning Harriet Powers's quilts within the lineage of the African American preaching tradition. Moving beyond the explicit rhetorical genre of preaching, as well as subverting the power and privilege of the pulpit often present in Black church preaching traditions, McCray asserts that the quilts crafted by the hands of Harriet Powers are more than folk art and an offering in visual arts: They are preaching. McCray connects Powers's artistry to the critical aspect of African American preaching known as "telling the story." Powers's use of imagination and elaboration as markers of the story also place her within the African American preaching tradition.

The significance of McCray's argument for this book is multifaceted. First, Powers is a Black woman whose quilt preaching is in an extracanonical homiletical form that would not readily or formally be understood as preaching by those who see preaching as solely pulpit practice and rhetorical art. The significance also lies in Powers's own declaration that her quilts were preaching. According to McCray, "Powers takes an unusual step by linking her quilting to preaching. She calls her first quilt 'a sermon in patchwork' and shares an intention to 'preach the gospel in patchwork, to show my Lord my humility . . . and to show where sin originated out of the beginning of things.'"[46] McCray did not name Powers as a preacher; Harriet Powers had already done that for herself. Powers's self-proclaimed orientation was that she was a preacher, and her works were sermons. For non-pulpit preachers, the affirmation of call comes first from themselves. Powers responds to that call with her quilts, and McCray posits that although it is not oral Powers finds a way to preach. When considered in its fullness, Black women's preaching demonstrates that sermonic discourse must be considered beyond the pulpit, and in Powers's case even beyond the orality of speech. For Powers and McCray, preaching is not just what we say orally. Preaching is not solely an oral/aural art form that requires auditory breath and physical voice in order to reach a gathered group of hearers. McCray shows the cleverness of Black women to work with what they have and to find ways to create lasting messages beyond the confines of pulpit practice and Sunday morning. She pushes homiletics beyond the pulpit, inviting and almost fighting for her reader to imagine a world beyond stagnant ideas of the genre of preaching. I, too, join in that same fight.

Homiletical Practice Beyond the Norm: A Liturgio-Ethic

For Black women non-pulpit preachers, preaching is a spiritual act that is also both a political and moral act, shaping the tenor of moral discourse in communities. In *Speaking Together and with God: Liturgy and Communicative Ethics*, John McClure uses his own coding system to consider confessional, intercessory, and homiletical practices through the lens of communicative ethics.[47] Liturgical practices have social impact and operate beyond the private sector and into the broader public sphere, McClure argues, writing, "Making such an argument requires that we understand liturgical practices to have a social life beyond confessional communities of faith, within public discourse and action."[48] This type of public discourse promotes a communicative ethic that focuses on understanding, not solely for the purposes of moral consensus but for the consideration of new moral norms that might expand the audience's perspective. If liturgical practices can be a means by which communicative action operates in the public sphere, then such practices are not limited to formalized pulpits and institutionally bound confessional spaces.[49]

To further his point, McClure highlights research on public moral artifacts that he considers homiletical based upon the aforementioned criteria of the four codes, or "four discursive practices."[50] McClure's contribution is the assertion that the core elements of homiletical practices can contribute to how a current moral consensus is problematized and a new valid moral consensus is discovered, authenticated, and argued as true.[51] Black women non-pulpit preachers use their rhetoric to fight against a moral consensus that is violent. They preach to intentionally disrupt the normative systems in order to create change towards a more just, free, and hospitable society for Black people, and they expand religious spheres into new public spaces through their preaching.

Conclusion: A Homiletical Intervention Through Black Women Non-Pulpit PreacHers

Homiletical artifacts are already present in everyday spaces, cultural spaces, and public spaces, yet so many preaching voices go unnoticed and unheard because of a limited scope of what preaching is. Black women non-pulpit preachers have been deemed speakers and orators without any study of the preaching component of their orality. However, as we study their specific goals, the exigencies to which they are responding, and the ways their intersections inform their preaching practice, the definition and purpose of preaching expands. The intersection of being Black and a woman, along with the places that these women chose to inhabit, push us to consider a new definition of preaching, which reshapes not only our contemporary practice but our understanding of the historical lineage of preaching.

In this chapter, I have outlined the lacunae in scholarship that have made it possible for the canon of preaching to have focused primarily on pulpit preachers. In *The Gendered Pulpit*, Mountford asks three questions that guide her work. She says, "What does it mean for a field of knowledge to take into consideration the experience of women? In what ways is a speech act or rhetorical performance 'gendered'? How does a woman earn the respect of an audience conditioned to regard her body itself as symbolic of lack (of authority, eloquence, power, substance)?"[52] To this line of inquiry I add, How does the specificity of Black women's preaching experiences reframe and expand our definitions of preaching and our methodological frameworks for the study of preaching? How does the way that preaching has historically been studied reinforce a definition that is limited and exclusive? These questions create a foundation for new preachers to be uncovered and spaces to be reimagined.

Sojourner Truth (1797–1883), Nannie Helen Burroughs (1879–1961), and Fannie Lou Hamer (1917–77) are the subjects of my study because I see them as preachers who push against the dominant locale of the pulpit for preaching, even as their preaching practice confirms and affirms some of the ideas of Black preaching, feminist preaching, and womanist preaching. Their aim to create better worlds and wield agency through their rhetoric—subversive to society around them—opens up a different telos for preaching than one might find in the pulpit. They advocated for freedom for their communities and asked for change as a response to their sermons.

Black women's non-pulpit preaching provides a new lens to view preaching and another place to explore the expansive nature of homiletics. It is rooted in Black hermeneutics yet centered in the Black community whose lives are both within and beyond the four walls of Black churches. These women were rooted in communities and created a homiletic deeply relevant to the issues and needs important to them and those around them. These women certainly had weary throats, yet they did the difficult work of using words to imagine and create worlds into which they called their community to live. Whether they were challenging white supremacy, inviting their own Black community into communal work or care, or speaking directly to systems of power, these women preached in a way that created change. The following chapters are a practice of listening to their preaching through their stories in order to glean insights about what preaching is outside of the pulpit and how we might practice and know preaching differently as a result of having engaged Sojourner Truth, Nannie Helen Burroughs, and Fannie Lou Hamer.

2
A Journey to Truth
The Life and Preaching Practice of Sojourner Truth

"You read books; God himself talks to me."[1]

"My name was Isabella; but when I left the house of bondage, I left everything behind. I wa'n't goin' to keep nothing of Egypt on me, an' so I went to the Lord an' asked him to give me a new name."[2] Sojourner Truth, originally named Isabella Baumfree, changed her name at a critical moment in her journey towards a new identity of freedom—freedom into which she had not been born. She declared her call to proclaim truth and that her name signified a journey given to her by God. For her, that was the only source of validation needed. This is the root of the preaching legacy of Sojourner Truth, whose preaching required no specific platform: just a sense of call, her story, and the urgent needs of the time to which she responded through her preaching.

By deepening our understanding of Sojourner Truth through her story, we learn that her rhetoric is rooted in the layers of her story. When we listen more fully to her life next to her language, we can see more fully that who she was informed what she proclaimed. In two of her homiletical artifacts—"Arn't I a Woman?" and "I Suppose I Am About the Only Colored Woman That Goes About to Speak for the Rights of Colored Women"—we encounter four homiletical insights drawn from the particularities of her rhetoric as a Black woman non-pulpit preacher in the nineteenth century.

In both of these messages, Truth was preaching at women's conventions where the focus was on women's rights, mostly geared towards the rights of white women. Despite using the term *women*, the proceedings often didn't include formerly enslaved, currently enslaved, or free Black women who were also women in the United States. Although Truth is not always named a preacher nor her rhetorical artifacts named as sermons, I listen to her rhetoric as preaching. Truth's preaching offers us strategies of tactical self-disclosure, metacommunication, cultivation of expansive biblical memory, and clarity of message geared at response. As a preacher focused on abolition and women's rights, she shows us the unique ways that non-pulpit preachers use their platforms to craft rhetoric deeply rooted in context with an explicit telos in mind, opening new ways of thinking for anyone who had a chance to hear her.

Her-Story: Sojourner Truth

Sojourner Truth's story is one of resilience, courage, and pivot points.[3] For many, her known story starts and ends with her activism, with some reference to her previous enslavement. However, her story was far more layered. Fortunately, Sojourner Truth did something unprecedented: She published her own narrative and sold it as a means of income when she spoke at conventions. Although she wasn't able to write or read, she told her narrative in a series of vignettes to her colleague Olive Gilbert, who transcribed them. However, the *Narrative* telling of her life ends before her speaking engagements proliferated. While we know some of Truth's story beyond her published narrative, Nell Irvin Painter concedes, "I cannot track completely Truth's antislavery and women's rights appearance, for reporters did not invariably consider her worth identifying by name, or even mentioning at all. She doubtless attended and addressed many meetings without notice between 1845 and 1850."[4] With that in mind, and in order to amplify the intersectional historical exigency of her public speaking, I tell her story, highlighting particularly pivotal moments.

Isabella Baumfree

Sojourner Truth, born in 1797 and named Isabella Baumfree, was the daughter of James and Elizabeth Baumfree.[5] She was born enslaved to a Dutch-speaking family in Ulster, New York. She witnessed pain and sorrow from a very young age. In the *Narrative of Sojourner Truth*, she talks about witnessing her parents' emotions as she and her siblings were sold or were under threat that they would be taken from each other. Baumfree saw deep love between her parents, saying, "Their human hearts beat within them with as true an affection as ever caused a human heart to beat."[6] However, she also watched and experienced immense grief. Baumfree recounts the agony and helplessness that her father experienced after her mother passed, reporting the effect his audible cries had on her: "I hear it now and remember it as well as if it were but yesterday. . . . My heart bled within me at the sight of his misery."[7] After her mother passed, her father lived in deep sorrow. Even when she saw him after she had been sold to another plantation, her experiences of him remained the same. Baumfree's familial narrative was rife with pain, as many of her siblings were sold off to different places and she, too, was sold from her parents.

While she was enslaved, Truth experienced physical, mental, emotional, and sexual abuse from the masters who enslaved her, as well as from their wives. At age nine, Baumfree was sold to John Neely for $100 and taken away from the plantation where her parents were. After having spoken only Dutch in the household into which she was born, she was thrust into an English-speaking household and had to adjust and learn a new language. Neely was violent and severely abused Baumfree. She describes a beating she received that left a "story" on her back that she would always have to remember: "He whipped her till the flesh was deeply lacerated and the blood streamed from her wounds—and the scars remain to the present day, to testify to the fact."[8] Soon after this, Baumfree was sold to the Scriveners for $150, and finally to John J. Dumont for £70. Baumfree was with the Dumonts from 1810 to 1826 (roughly age thirteen to twenty-nine).

Both Baumfree and her biographers emphasize her time with the Dumonts. She had a deeply complicated relationship with the family. Painter writes, "[Baumfree] denounced Sally Dumont [slave master's wife], adored John Dumont, and converted to a recognition that slavery was wrong."[9] In her *Narrative*, Baumfree speaks highly of the Dumonts' daughter Gertrude, who helped her when her mistress and a white woman servant told a lie about her to John Dumont in order to get her in trouble. Baumfree also had a high ambition and desire to please Dumont. Painter writes, "Her ambition and desire to please were so great that she often worked several nights in succession, sleeping only short snatches, as she sat in her chair; and some nights she would not allow herself to take any sleep, save what she could get resting herself against the wall, fearing that if she sat down, she would sleep too long."[10] Fellow slaves taunted her, calling her "white folks' nigger."[11] Her relationship with the Dumonts was complicated because of its inherent distortions and misplaced affection, rooted in the abuse and mishandling of her person.

One of the ways that the enslaved were controlled was through their relationships. Truth experienced deep heartbreak from losing a lover. Agency for love was not often given to the enslaved, especially when a couple came from different owners. Baumfree speaks of a critical time when she fell in love with an enslaved man named Robert from another plantation. Like many enslaved persons, Baumfree was the victim of cruel separation and was not able to see him. Robert's master didn't want his slaves with anyone else. When it was found out that Robert had come to see Baumfree, he was beaten so severely that her master, Dumont, intervened and made the owners who were beating Robert leave. "Isabella had witnessed this scene from her window," writes Painter, "and was greatly shocked at the murderous treatment of poor Robert, whom she truly loved, and whose only crime, in the eye of his persecutors, was his affection for her."[12] Throughout her life, she saw that others' affection for her and/or care for herself were often met with punishment and persecution. Eventually she was pressured to marry Thomas, a fellow slave on her plantation, and they had five children.

In addition to the loss of someone she loved and who loved her, Baumfree also experienced the loss of her children. After she left for her own freedom, laws still bound her children to her previous owners, the Dumonts. However, the Dumonts also made an illegal sale of her son Peter. Increasing her pain and fear, Baumfree discovered that Peter had been sold "down south," which for many Northern slaves added an additional layer of terror. Baumfree worked to get Peter back and was helped by others to locate him and return him to her. When she finally was able to get him, he didn't recognize her; he had been brainwashed with ideas of who she was and told that she was evil. He even expressed that he wanted to stay with his enslaver. After some time, Baumfree was able to get Peter to see that she was his mother who fought for him and had come to find him. He then began to tell her all that had happened, and "she commenced as soon as practicable to examine the boy, and found to her utter astonishment that from the crown of his head to the sole of his foot, the callosities and indurations on his entire body were most frightful to behold."[13] Her pain was profound as a human and as a mother who couldn't protect her son from what had happened. She had prayed for him to return, and he had—but not without the external and internal scars of abuse and terrorizing treatment. This type of treatment was a stripping of her rights as a human being, but the enslaved weren't seen as having rights. Her story is reflected in her fight for women's rights and in her proclaiming, because she intimately knew what it was like to have no rights both as an enslaved person and now as a freed Black woman. Through her preaching, she emphasized those rights and she fought for better treatment.

Towards Freedom

Freedom was not something given to Baumfree; it was something that she took. On July 4, 1827, Baumfree was supposed to receive her freedom from the Dumonts, but John Dumont refused, saying that he had lost labor from her because of an injury she sustained, and therefore she would not be emancipated.[14] In her *Narrative*, she recounts a conversation with God where she said that she was afraid of the night and wondered how she could escape. She was guided by the Spirit to leave before daybreak so that she wouldn't travel completely in the dark but would be away from familiar neighborhoods before anyone else was up. She left with her infant and the clothes that she had.[15] She escaped and encountered the Van Wagners, who bought her labor from Dumont for a year until she could fully advocate for and claim her freedom.[16] Her escape marked a change in her identity. She decided in that moment to fight for her freedom in a different way, which would continue to be a theme across her life—and one that appeared in her rhetoric as well. Her preaching was a continued fight for this freedom. It wasn't enough for her to have paperwork that said she was free; she knew she deserved to have the same rights as the people around her. The fight for freedom was a theme throughout Truth's life as she advocated for more rights and believed God had sent her to do this work.

Religious Radicalism

After Baumfree left the Dumonts, she connected to a religious movement called Perfectionism and was taken in by Elijah Pierson and his wife, both preachers in the tradition.[17] She participated in the movement in various ways, including preaching at camp meetings alongside the other families.[18] In October 1832, Baumfree met Robert Matthews, who was more commonly known as the Prophet Matthias. He was a self-proclaimed prophet, foretelling that the end of the world would be in 1836. He dressed ornately, adorned with things like a two-edged sword and different astrological devices.[19] As Painter describes, "Matthias claimed that after the Spirit of Truth had disappeared from the earth with the death of Matthias of the New Testament, he, the Prophet Matthias, possessed the spirits of both Matthias and Jesus Christ."[20]

When Matthias arrived, the Perfectionists believed him: Pierson rented a house for him, and Baumfree served as his housekeeper without compensation. In addition, she gave money from her savings to support the work that he was doing. The Kingdom of Matthias "consisted of different generations, classes, races, and sexes; Isabella was the only one who was black, but not the only one who was poor."[21] Although in the previous Perfectionist movement Baumfree had been given space to preach, Matthias said that preaching wasn't for women. He cut off her voice and exploited her labor and generosity. Matthias was abusive and domineering, but because of their religious adherence the group continued to follow him. Ann Folger, the wife of Matthias, also sexually abused Isabella, coming into her bed at night, which was reminiscent of a previous mistress, Sally Dumont.[22] These experiences mimicked the treatment she had received as an enslaved person, yet in this group she felt a different proximity to whiteness than she had experienced as a slave. The Kingdom of Matthias fell apart when his indiscretions became public knowledge. Baumfree stuck by him for much of that time, using her resources to support him and enduring mocking from others who couldn't understand why. However, her loyalty diminished over time, and she became more disillusioned by what had happened.[23]

When reflecting on this time in the Kingdom of Matthias, Truth speaks of being in a liminal space between colleague and servant, which created ambiguity and confusion in her roles. What was clear, however, was that her status as Black, woman, and poor deeply shaped how she was treated and considered within the household—as had been true throughout her life. Truth saw the ways that the particularities of her embodiment created a different experience than that of any of her counterparts who didn't share the layers of identity impacting her. This season of life provided her with the opportunity to listen to different interpretations of Scripture and exploration of her own theological identity, which she then mobilized in her later preaching by using the biblical texts to support her call for rights and freedom.

Sojourner Truth

After her experience in the Kingdom of Matthias, Baumfree left New York City. On June 1, 1843, which was Pentecost, she changed her name from Isabella Baumfree to Sojourner Truth: "She informed Mrs. Whiting, the woman of the house where she was stopping, that her name was no longer Isabella, but SOJOURNER; and that she was going east. And to her inquiry, 'What are you going east for?' her answer was, 'the Spirit calls me there, and I must go.'"[24] This name change was significant because in slavery she had been given a name, and changing it herself marked a new sense of freedom and living alongside the Spirit and into her call. She recognized the importance of a name and the ways that it signified who she was claiming to be. Her name change was an act of reclaiming herself as one where truth lives, and as a person who expresses truth wherever she proclaims. Again, Sojourner Truth chose another level of freedom for herself and worked to lean into this new stage of her life more fully. Her sense of call brought her to Connecticut. The power and resiliency to choose to be something else in a world that had tried to place her in a particular box and social location is significant. This pivot in her narrative is critical as we consider her preaching. Her preaching was rooted in her life story, with a goal of justice and more rights. She knew too intimately the consequences of lack of rights, and her preaching was focused on fighting for rights for women generally, including those often excluded: Black women.

Proclaiming Truth

Sojourner Truth was known widely as an activist and speaker; however, there aren't a lot of manuscripts of her preaching. We do know that some of the presentations of her proclamations were adapted by others for particular audiences and were not true to her actual rhetoric. In one of her most famous proclaiming moments, known popularly as "Ain't I a Woman?" (but we now know it to be "Arn't I a Woman?"), disparities between the original and later presentations are vast. Marius Robinson's report of the meeting, published in the *Anti-Slavery Bugle*, is crucial for distinguishing these differences.[25] He was Truth's friend and host, and recorded what she said in her own vernacular, instead of the reimagined vernacular that would become the popular memory of the speech. Painter writes, "Robinson introduces Truth as an ex-slave, but without the use of dialect or other rhetorical techniques to emphasize her blackness. . . . According to Robinson, Truth did not seize the floor, she asked permission to speak; and as though doubting her right, she announced that her intervention will be brief."[26] By contrast, Frances Gage later published another record in the *New York Independent* that differed from the original manuscript and was written in a Southern dialect that would not have been true to Truth's speaking.[27]

It is crucial, then, to note that the legend of Truth and the life of Truth are disparate. Certain people wanted Truth to demonstrate a particular performance of Blackness that simply wasn't true to her; her rhetoric was manipulated to form a palatable manuscript that reinforced the icon she had become, rather than the actual person she was or an accurate account of her words.[28] Her actual words are enough. Too often Black women are made to be icons, aunties, and legends, and the overall narrative of their lives—including both difficulties and triumphs—get overlooked because of a need for them to fit into a simplistic category. Truth knew and expressed that her story was her own, and not all of it was meant for public consumption. With that in mind, and knowing the care she took with language, what she did share publicly through proclamation or personal storytelling was both intentional and precise. Within the words of Sojourner Truth are rooted the very real experiences of Isabella Baumfree.[29] The aim of this book is to listen to her preaching to discover what her homiletic teaches us.

Introduction to the Artifacts

The following section offers a detailed consideration of two of Truth's sermons, both offered at conventions: "Arn't I a Woman?"[30] preached at the Women's Convention in Akron, Ohio, in 1851,[31] and "I Suppose I Am About the Only Colored Woman That Goes About to Speak for the Rights of Colored Women" (hereafter "I Suppose"),[32] preached in 1853 in New York City at the Fourth

National Women's Rights Convention. Each of these moments was extemporaneous and invites us to consider preaching insights and invitations through the proclamation of Sojourner Truth.

Homiletical Insights

The Sacred Self: Tactical Self-Disclosure

The first homiletical insight is *tactical self-disclosure*. Truth used her experiences to enhance her messages and yet was clear that she did not have to share every detail from her story with everyone. Even in her *Narrative*, she was particular about what she shared. In the *Narrative*, Olive Gilbert writes,

> There are some hard things that crossed Isabella's life while in slavery that she has no desire to publish, for various reasons. 1. She was protecting the people who were in relationship with those who caused the pain, because she didn't believe that they needed to be injured by the truth of their beloved. 2. Because they are not all for the public ear. 3. She says, were she to tell all that happened to her as a slave—all that she knows is "God's truth"—it would seem to others, especially the uninitiated, so unaccountable, so unreasonable, and what is usually called so unnatural . . . they would not easily believe it.[33]

This shows that for her, the particularities of her narrative were a tactic to move towards a message and an invitation. They were also a mark of agency, detailing what she wanted to take with her and what she chose to leave behind for others to know. Storytelling was critical—not only for the sake of testifying, but for drawing out a demand for her hearers. However, her storytelling also marked her agency in disclosing only what she decided was pertinent.

One execution of tactical self-disclosure occurred through her chosen name and her decision to come into public spaces as Sojourner Truth, not Isabella Baumfree. Renaming (re-signifying, re-imagining, re-identifying) herself was critical for Truth because her previous name was attached to her enslavement. When Isabella Baumfree decided to rename, she honored her agency to be *who she was called to be*, not who she had been told she was.[34] This didn't mean that she didn't carry her story with her; rather, she was choosing to live out a different narrative with a type of agency. For Truth, it was actually changing her name that signified her freedom from enslavement and from the bonds of anyone else (like Matthias) who would try to control her. Through this move, Truth invites Black women, who have not been at the center of homiletical practices, to consider the power of a name and/or self-identification in our homiletical practice. This rhetorical change notes agency and can be an invitation for preachers and proclaimers to decide what they want to be called in order to state most clearly who they are deciding to be.

The other more explicit way that Truth utilized this strategy was through using important moments of her story as a means to deliver her overall message. In "Arn't I a Woman?" Truth opens her first section with examples of her work in the fields. She recounts, "I have as much muscle as any man, and can do as much work as any man. I have plowed and reaped and husked and chopped and mowed, and can any man do more than that? I have heard much about the sexes being equal. I can carry as much as any man, and eat as much, too, if I can get it. I am as strong as any man that is now."[35] Without naming it explicitly, she shows that she is Black, woman, and poor. She is describing the work of enslaved people and/or those on plantations as free Blacks who still had to work these specific jobs. This point is critical because most white women weren't doing these jobs. By doing some self-exegesis in the form of rhetorical prose, Truth asks the audience to consider that if she is equal to men in all these ways that are characteristic of an enslaved person (which again distinguishes her from her white women counterparts), then she should have equal rights. She also says, "I can't read, but I can hear."[36] Again, a part of her story is being denied access to literacy. She names this but also points out that it doesn't stop her from having something to say. This use of narrative in small sound bites offers enough to round out who she is without a longer, detailed narrative of her life.

In "I Suppose," Truth says, "I come to you, citizens of New York; I was born in it, and I was a slave in the state of New York; and now I am a good citizen of this state."[37] She discloses her history of slavery and being free, and her place as a citizen. Enslaved people weren't citizens, Black people historically have not been given their full rights as citizens, freed or otherwise, and Black women weren't often thought of as citizens at all in their particularity. By beginning the sermon with these declarations, Truth sets up her hearer to consider her experience as support for her message. This is different from including experiences with which the audience would identify. Instead, she is speaking from the particularity of how her experience diverges from theirs.

Metacommunication

The second homiletical insight from Truth's preaching is *metacommunication.* Truth was metacommunicative about hegemonic ideologies that were active in the context where her message was received. She named explicitly that being a Black woman in the spaces in which she was proclaiming made her words feel different to her hearers because her embodiment was not one they were used to seeing. Revealing what was clearly present created an opportunity for those listening to examine why it was so strange, even as she then proceeded to declare and name the importance of the rights she was asking for.

In "Arn't I a Woman?" Truth declares, "I am a woman's rights."[38] She doesn't say, "I have women's rights," or "I should have women's rights." She declares her place using an "I am" within the system in which she is denied a full identity. She is saying, therefore, Your denial of my rights is not something to be taken lightly or outside of the context of my humanity; you are attempting to deny me my actual self by taking away what is mine. Specifically, for Truth, whose background was littered with abuse, mishandling, enslavement, and oppression, to publicly declare her humanity was subversive to societal and theological norms riddled with patriarchy and racism. Her use of "I am" situates her as an embodiment of what she was asking for, a Black woman, which was not the normative, white woman's embodiment associated with the women's rights movement in the nineteenth century.

In "I Suppose" Truth explicitly names what may be keeping the hearer from receiving her message. She asserts, "I know that it feels o' hissin' and ticklin' to see a colored woman get up and tell you about these things, and Woman's Rights."[39] This strategy shows that Truth knows that it is peculiar for her hearers that she is speaking. Crowds at these events were used to hearing white women (and the occasional white man) speak. She names that she is talking about and advocating for women's rights, and then immediately afterward points out that this messaging is different for people to hear from her as a Black woman. The clarity and plainness of her words are important: Women's rights matter *and* Black rights matter, because I, a Black woman, deserve rights. Truth also proclaims, "We have all been thrown down so low that nobody thought that we'd ever get up again; but we have been long enough trodden now; we will come up again, and now I am here."[40] *I am here.* Truth states that she is here in a space that, based on her experience, she knows she is not "supposed" to be, and yet she is here and advocating for a better situation for herself and others like her.

Disrupting normative discourse through metacommunicative rhetoric positioned Truth, in the specifics of her embodiment, to preach the particular messages of justice from her perspective. This was also a strategy of claiming space in a place that would often ignore the very intersections she was emphasizing. While we don't have many records of the audience's reaction to Truth's rhetoric, one can imagine that in a time when white women activists were pushing Truth to speak on women's rights without focusing on color, and Black men were pushing her towards solidarity with the cause of abolition without considering her womanhood, her declaration of "both/and" created a new paradigm for her hearers. Truth's prose brings to light a triple consciousness that evokes for her hearers a new consciousness about the nuances of women's rights and expectations for Black women.[41]

Interpreting Texts: Cultivating Expansive Biblical Memory

Sojourner Truth engaged the practice of *cultivating expansive memory*, both biblically and theologically, to include the oppression of Black people and women and the ways that those identities intersect. Her preaching intertwines her experience and her exposition of Scripture in a dance that adds her voice to the exegetical rendering of the text. She invites her audience into a practice of remembering the world of the biblical text through the lens of her experience and does so with one aim in mind: change towards justice. The audience hears how the stories of Black women disrupt the ways the text has been read to maintain the status quo. Truth's life as a preacher was grounded in the work of justice, and her re-membering of Scripture in her preaching was used towards that end as well.[42]

In "Arn't I a Woman?" Truth draws on the Bible as a foundation to justify her fight for women's rights, centering the experiencing of Black women. Through her own interpretive lens, she expands the normative readings of the text by centering the women and reading them generously. For example, she says, "I have heard the Bible and learned that Eve caused man to sin. Well if woman upset the world, do give her a chance to set it right side up again."[43] She was known for sarcasm, and she utilized the Bible as a tool to unveil nonsensical logic: Even if it is true that Eve caused sin, advocacy for women's rights is advocacy for a chance to make right what is wrong.[44] She then goes to Mary, Martha, and Jesus: "When Lazarus died, Mary and Martha came to him with faith and love and besought him to raise their brother. And Jesus wept, and Lazarus came forth."[45] Jesus responded to the requests of women, and "he never spurned woman from him."[46] Jesus came to them when Lazarus died and helped them when they called, which is what she was asking people to do in her speech. As a final point, Truth reminds her hearers that this same Jesus did not come from man at all but "through God who created him and a woman who bore him. Man, where is your part?"[47] This walk through the Scripture, from Adam and Eve to Jesus's life to the very existence of Jesus, recalls the text in order to make one point: Women have rights, and the fact that men are keeping them from this is antibiblical, anti-God, and antihuman. In this, she is promoting, deepening, and expanding the intertextuality of anamnesis among her listeners, encouraging them to remember the myriad ways that women's rights appear in the text in stories that would have been familiar to many of the hearers.[48] Her use of Scripture disrupts the hearer's perception of women's rights and claims those rights as something everyone needs to address.

In "I Suppose" Truth uses Scripture to create a historical precedent for the request that she was making. Truth says, "I was a-thinkin', when I see women contendin' for their rights, I was a-thinkin' what a difference there is now and what there was in old times. I have only a few minutes to speak; but in the old times the kings of earth would hear a woman."[49] She is paralleling the "old times" and her contemporary moment in order to say, So what is happening now? She then goes on to talk about Esther.[50] "Queen Esther come forth, for she was oppressed, and felt there was a great wrong, and she said I will die or I will bring my complaint before the king. Should the king of the United States be greater or more crueler or more harder?"[51] She talks about what the king did for Esther and wonders aloud why women in her own context are treated as "less than." She draws a parallel for the audience to consider: If this is the ideal that we see from the text, what then is our right or prerogative to operate in another fashion? Truth asserts, "The women want their rights as Esther."[52] Her identity and her explicit inclusion of Black women through naming her own presence in her sermon leaves no question about whether or not she is including Black women in the necessity of rights that are justified by the text. Her reference back to her context via the text creates a solid parallel. Following these things, Truth draws on Jesus's words in Matthew 13:37, saying, "What I say to one, I say to all—watch!" because what was said to men is also given to women. Then, drawing on Exodus 20:12, which says, "Honor your father and mother," she pushes against the ways that children are mocking their mothers for the audacity to speak up and claim their rights. Again, Truth uses the text to condemn what is happening in her current context.

Truth quilted together her knowledge as a strategy for her message. She spoke of "women" in general and expanded the audience's memory of biblical women, such as Esther, as authoritative prototypes. Yet by talking about herself as a colored woman and from the beginning naming ways that colored women had been pushed down, Truth included Black women explicitly—not as an addendum to the movement—in the narrative of women's rights and in the legitimating anamnesis of biblical women. When we hear Queen Esther's story in this sermon, there's an interplay between this woman who just claimed her New York citizenship and her experiences of oppression and declared space, which stands alongside this biblical witness of a woman doing the same. We have Sojourner Truth's narrative of standing in front of people who would be shocked to hear her because "colored women" wouldn't have gotten that platform, set alongside Queen Esther, who showed up to the table to speak. These texts dance with each other to promote a remembering of the text that works alongside a remembering and acknowledging of Black women's particular experiences, as seen through Truth's story.

Clarity of Message for Response

The final homiletical insight gleaned from Sojourner Truth's proclaiming is a clarity of message for the purpose of a clear request for response. She oscillates between assertive and conversational truths to keep the possibilities for her hearer's response open while maintaining an explicit end goal.[53] The aim is clear: women's rights, which must include Black women. Sojourner Truth spoke because her message was urgent. Her aim was to evoke an actionable response in which all people—but specifically men, more specifically white men—would be more adherent and attentive to women's rights, and especially her rights as a Black woman. Truth invokes her rights by intentionally proclaiming that she is a woman, and therefore to deny those rights to her is to deny her actual self. As a previously enslaved woman, she has experienced even fewer rights in the past, and yet she remains in constant and immediate danger and is denied access to things that others have. Truth's message pushes a particular moral discourse into the public sphere, using cultural references to affirm her equality and reiterate the urgent need for change.[54] Truth's preaching responds to a hierarchical society in which white women were seen as having less value than white men, Black men less than white women, and Black women less than Black men. For Truth, naming the importance of women's rights and why they were necessary was a goal that couldn't be convoluted or misinterpreted. When the message is urgent, inductive approaches aren't as effective because you are dependent on the hearer receiving and interpreting them. Instead, "making it plain" is an effective strategy in Truth's preaching.

In "Arn't I a Woman?"[55] Truth's message is that it is dangerous for those withholding women's rights to do so, and thus women should be given their rights. First, she appeals to logic and sarcastically uses the image of measuring amounts (pints and quarts) to talk about rights: "As for intellect, all I can say is, if woman have a pint, and man a quart—why can't she have her little pint full? You need not be afraid to give us our rights for fear we will take too much, for we can't take more than one pint will hold."[56] At the end of the section she proclaims, "Why children, if you have a woman's right[s], give it to her and you will feel better," suggesting that these rights are not yours to keep for yourself, and if you are carrying them you probably feel "off" because you are holding what doesn't belong to you.[57] She is claiming that those holding and withholding the rights of other people are the ones in the spot of danger. Truth names the ramifications of ignoring her request: "But man is in a tight place, the poor slave is on him, woman is coming on him, he is surely between a hawk and a buzzard."[58] This sentence is particularly interesting because Truth herself is both the slave and the woman, the hawk and the buzzard, Black and woman. This is the thesis: Give *all* women their rights. This thesis came with a warning for those who refused, that they would be the ones in danger because the rights were going to come.

In "I Suppose," Truth is still focused on women's rights and making clear what she is requesting. Her message is that women should receive their rights, and they aren't asking for much. She reiterates, "I come forth to speak 'bout Woman's Rights . . . ,"[59] and continues, "We'll have our rights; see if we don't; and you can't stop us from them; see if you can."[60] This sermon is later than "Arn't I a Woman?" yet it keeps the same clarity about what she is here to talk about and why. Because she was speaking at women's rights conventions, it wasn't necessary for her to name her topic directly. Yet for the sake of posterity, she makes it clear that as a Black woman she is advocating for the rights of her people—women and Black people—and doing so in a space for women's rights.

Truth also places heavy emphasis on the ability of human beings to act and move, declaring that women's rights are not something that has to be a controversial issue. Rights can be given, things can change, and therefore they should. In both of the artifacts looked at here, Truth does suggest that should human beings *not* act—specifically the men she is calling forth to respond—then God will. In "Arn't I a Woman?" Truth says, "But the women are coming up blessed by God and a few men are coming up with them."[61] God is already moving, and you can get on the side of the blessed if you participate in making right that which is wrong. This statement affirms that God is on the side of those who are struggling and oppressed, and God's hand is working through them.

Conclusion

Sojourner Truth preached at a time when Black people, especially Black women, were not regarded as humans but as labor. She advocated for the rights of women and Black people, showing up in her body as both. Across her proclaiming moments, her preaching consistently opened new perspectives for her hearers and asked for a clear response. Four important homiletical strategies are visible in Sojourner Truth's preaching. These homiletical strategies emerge from hearing Truth through intersectional exigency: the demand on her particularity and how she responds rhetorically. Truth's preaching makes rhetorical use of *tactical self-disclosure*, *metacommunication*, *cultivating expansive biblical memory*, and *clarity of message for response*. Each of these homiletical tactics emerges from the particularity of her preaching identity as a Black woman non-pulpit preacher, shaped through the rhythms of her story, in order to meet head on the urgent needs of the times and places where she speaks.

In Sojourner Truth's preaching, her tactical self-disclosure is at work alongside her cultivation of expansive memory in the biblical text. Her experience plays alongside the biblical text to support her messaging around her rights, and therefore the possibility of women's flourishing within society. In his exposition of a "transformational" hermeneutic of Scripture in *The Four Codes of Preaching*, McClure writes, "The transformational style is correct in showing that, having discovered the truth claims of the biblical text, we must not leave them like 'the assertions dissected in the classrooms of logic' but enable them to 'reach us at the level of deep affect and make a personal claim upon us.'"[62] It is the interplay between Truth's lived experience, which is different than that of most of her hearers, and her reading of the Scriptures that gives the actual affect. Truth doesn't just use her experience to support the biblical text, but her experience becomes a "text" of its own, read and revealed as its own revelation for what is to come. She knows that her audience is full of people without her experience but familiar enough to know the reasons her experience is shaped in particular ways. Therefore, by revealing her experience and allowing others into the nuances of what it means to be poor, Black, and woman, she speaks from that place and asserts her focus, marking precedent with the biblical text.

For Sojourner Truth, the message was clear because it had to be. Men, grant women their rights, and while we're at it, white men specifically, grant Black people their rights, too. She draws attention to her embodiment with semantic clarity; her message includes all of who she is, which is neither just woman nor just Black, and which is also supported by her experience as a previously enslaved Black woman. Truth's commitment to a clear message as a response to exigent needs offers perspective on what kind of rhetorical tools are used when the necessity for clarity is urgent. She was there to talk about, advocate for, and make claims about the deserved rights of Black women and invite the hearers to participate in extending those rights. This was socially and politically disruptive. She knew that, and instead of backing down, she used metacommunication to place her own body in the middle of her message, knowing that her very *presence* was disruptive to what was considered normative.

As stated previously, the women's rights movement at the time was dominated by white women. Truth was asked to speak specifically about women's rights, as if her rights as a Black person weren't inextricably bound to her rights as woman. The movement at large seemed to want her to show up as a Black woman to affirm the sameness of womanhood and remove the racial identity and class identity of being poor and formerly enslaved. In *Ingenuity*, Lisa Thompson writes, "Those who remain and render a message in places that would prefer their invisibility dare to preach with a distinct and creatively tactical imagination for the sake of their deep convictions—*ingenuity*."[63] To speak one's whole truth as a Black woman is not only an act of self-care but of community care, expanding the space for others whose persons are rendered societally invisible to speak as well. When Black women choose not to live in the identity fragments imposed on them by society, they display courage while affirming their own humanity. Truth's preaching demands space for her voice and the voices of those like her who aren't in the room, all of whom believe that their rights are worth fighting for. As Truth says, "We have all been thrown down so low that nobody thought we'd ever get up again; but we have been long enough trodden now; we will come up again, and now I am here."[64]

3
A Commitment to Black Women, a Belief in Black People
The Life and Preaching Practice of Nannie Helen Burroughs

> "Negroes should stop apologizing for not being white and rank their own race."[1]

"If you are going to be a Christian, you've got to do something week-days as well as talk and feel about it Sundays."[2] Nannie Helen Burroughs said this to her friend Rev. Earl Harrison as she was talking about what it meant to live as a Christian beyond weekly worship. Her work aimed at the everydayness of life, helping to elevate Black people through training and support. Burroughs was a prolific proclaimer, a renowned educator, and a woman committed to working tirelessly to support the upward movement of Black people during the early to mid-twentieth century. While she was deeply entrenched in the Baptist church at both a local and national level, her platforms for speaking were not Sunday morning worship services. Burroughs was extensively involved in organizations geared towards the betterment and support of Black women in the different spheres where they operated, which opened up more influence, more opportunity, and more training to support their efforts and their survival. For Burroughs, proclamation was a means to continue the practice of supporting Black women, not something confined to any specific platform or setting.

Ignited by God's call to service, Burroughs fortified her activism through her proclamation. While some aspects of her commitments may be contentious to the twenty-first-century reader because of the seeming adherence to gender norms of the time, her proclamation within the specificity of her time period was both radical and subversive in many ways. In addition, the reality that her work and words mattered and had a great impact cannot be argued. The initiatives she was able to complete through the money she raised for Black women's education and survival, and the organizations she created as places for Black women to have a voice and be supported in their flourishing, would be significant had she never spoken a word. However, her public rhetorical witness across different spheres—religious, educational, activist, and otherwise—wove these identities through all the spaces she inhabited. She knew these spheres intimately through her own experience and by watching her mother and her grandmother work to survive. In spite of all that she accomplished, she felt like she had not done enough to deserve accolades and praise. "In a letter to her friend Carter G. Woodson [in 1931, which was well after the school was running and she was established in the Women's Convention], Burroughs bemoaned a chapter about her in Sadie Daniel's *Women Builders* (1931) as premature: 'I have not done enough to be given a place in any book. I hope to accomplish something that will be enduring and really constructive, but up to now I am woefully disgusted with what I have been able to accomplish for the women and girls of my race.'"[3] She was always striving to do more and would not feel accomplished until she truly felt Black women at large had the resources they needed. Although people may call her different things—educator, leader, advocate, activist, speaker—she would most readily self-identify as one doing the work of the Lord. As a result, the biographical information on her early years is slim, because she felt that talking about herself was more trivial than using her time to speak about the causes and initiatives she supported.[4]

Different scholars have asked, Who is Nannie Helen Burroughs the person, the educator, the activist, and/or thinker? My question is, Who is Nannie Helen Burroughs the proclaimer, and what homiletical insights are we invited to consider through her preaching, which extended into so many different spheres? By walking with Nannie Helen Burroughs through the arc of her life alongside her proclamation, we see the ways her experiences ignited her sense of call and illumine the rhetorical threads that can be seen throughout her work. Two of her pieces—"How the Sisters Are Hindered from Helping" and "The Colored Woman and Her Relation to the Domestic Problem"—give us a depth of insight into her homiletic prowess and offer room to consider what homiletical insights can be drawn from her rhetoric. Homiletically, Burroughs encourages: (1) clarity of message as a response to exigency, (2) a salvific understanding of Black women's presence and participation within institutions, (3) scriptural and explicit God references as familiar taproots that attend closely to her context, and (4) language specific to the particular audience she was aiming to influence. Each of these homiletical emphases shows us something about Black women's homiletical strategies in spaces beyond the pulpit. These strategies arise from the particularity of Burroughs's experience and the rhetorical exigencies she confronted. She spent her life responding to the problems of Black women operating within ecclesiastical and social institutions and aimed to create more space for women's flourishing. Burroughs is known as many things, and preaching can be included in the list of practices she embodied.

Her-story: Nannie Helen Burroughs

Nannie Helen Burroughs intentionally avoided talking about her early life or her personal life. Her focus was on the work in front of her, which positioned her story within other stories, particularly the larger story of the Christian gospel. Although there are clear ties between her early life and her rhetoric, because of the lack of available details her story must be pieced together. Though her early years are significant, she began her public witness at only twenty-one years old, and the institutions she created and in which she participated constituted the bulk of her life and work.

What follows is a brief snapshot of her story, moving through her early life, her work with the National Baptist Convention, her creation of the National Training School for Girls, and finally her affiliations and work with several other organizations—all for the purposes of accomplishing God's work by helping Black women.

Burroughs was born in Virginia on May 2, 1879, to John Burroughs and Jennie Poindexter Burroughs. Her maternal grandfather was a former slave who, after he was freed, was able to own a small farm. Both her father and uncle were freed just before the Civil War began, and after the war ended, they were able to purchase land as well. This put their family on a better financial footing than other Black people at the time who were unable to own land and/or find stable income. John Burroughs was also a Baptist preacher who received some education from Richmond Institute.[5] While Burroughs knew her father in her early years, his presence wasn't consistent for the majority of her life. When Burroughs was five, her only sister, Maggie, died. After Maggie's death, Burroughs's mother took her to live in Washington, DC, with her maternal grandmother, where there were better educational opportunities for her. While in DC, Burroughs was an active youth at Nineteenth Street Baptist Church.[6]

Burroughs's mother and grandmother, who raised her, were critical role models in her life. In the few anecdotes we have from Burroughs, she often speaks of her mother, Jennie, and her grandmother, Maria. Jennie Burroughs was a domestic worker, and this position taught Burroughs firsthand the issues and vulnerabilities faced by a single Black woman trying to provide for her family in the late nineteenth century.[7] Her grandmother, Maria Poindexter, pushed Burroughs to live with honor and pride, regardless of what she was doing. She lived by the motto, "We ain't no hung-down-head race," and she instilled in her granddaughter "a deep sense of racial pride and an infinite respect for folk wisdom."[8] Poindexter said:

> Hold your spirit up inside, child, hold your spirit up and that helps you to hold your head up. Don't let your spirit down. I used to hold my head up so high that sometimes they

> would say, "Maria why don't you look down at the ground?" I would say, "look down at the ground? I aint no groundhog. I am looking up at God because that's what He made me for." Honey, they slaved my body, but they didn't slave my mind. I was thinking high, myself, and some day we colored folks is going to live high.[9]

The influences of both her mother and grandmother show up in Burroughs's work and her rhetoric. We see her respect for people who make an honest living and an emphasis on honor as salvific practice for Black people. Her commitment to education and excellence also stemmed from these roots of the women who raised her.

Burroughs's educational history is particularly important because she spent a large part of her later career in education, and her commitment to scholastic excellence began early. As a child, she had typhoid for two years, an experience that might have put others behind in school, but not Burroughs: She was able to graduate at seventeen alongside her original class.[10] She went to M Street High School, which is well known in DC for its illustrious history and faculty, and she graduated in 1896.[11] During high school, Burroughs organized the Harriet Beecher Stowe Literary Society, which gave students an opportunity for both literary and oratorical expression.[12] This practice of oratorical and literary work would continue in the school she later created. Upon graduating, Burroughs expected to find a job teaching in the Washington, DC, public school system but unfortunately was unable to do so. "It broke me up at first," Burroughs said. "I had my life all planned out, to settle down in Washington with my good mother, do that pleasant work, draw a good salary and be comfortable for the rest of my life."[13] This was a critical turning point for Burroughs because she had to figure out what to do now that all of her plans had led her to the classroom, and yet she did not get a teaching job, even though she was known to be excellent. Although this was a difficult moment for Burroughs, she persevered.

Burroughs's career after graduation included various jobs, but her goal of being an educator never faded. Through a family friend,

Burroughs landed a job at the *Christian Banner*, a Baptist paper. She was known to have excelled in that role; as her employer said, "We have never had her equal. She is a dynamo in an office. Her motto always was, 'Do a thing so thoroughly that no one else can improve on it.'"[14] After scoring highly on an exam, Burroughs tried to get a job as a clerk but was told there were no jobs for colored clerks and ended up working as a custodian in an office building. This was a short part of her story but greatly informed her later emphasis on honoring domestic occupations and helping Black women in their training. Sometime later, Burroughs became L. G. Jordan's bookkeeper and editorial secretary. He was the historian and corresponding secretary for the National Baptist Convention's Foreign Missions Board. Burroughs moved to Louisville with the National Baptist Convention when they established a new national office there in 1900. This was the beginning of the career for which Nannie Helen Burroughs is known. She spent the majority of her life doing work for Black Baptist women and Black women generally, both domestically and globally.

Burroughs's work with the National Baptist Convention (NBC) cannot be understated. The year she began her work alongside L. G. Jordan was also the year of her inaugural public proclamation, "How the Sisters Are Hindered from Helping." This was the catalyst for the vote that opened up opportunity for the Women's Convention (WC) to be established in 1900, a major accomplishment. Establishing the WC was not easy because the men of the NBC were reluctant to let women have their own sphere in which to operate. Virginia Broughton, Mary Cook, and Lucy Smith had been trying to get the WC going since 1880. In 1900 the WC was able to get more established and gain more traction, which were the fruits of the labor of the previous twenty years.[15] The main obstacle was the gender dynamic within the NBC in which men in power did not want to lose control of women's work by giving them their own sphere of operation. The men were primarily ministers and many of the women were their wives. The men didn't think their "helpmates" needed their own space, which brought up issues of power and submission.[16] However, in her proclamation Burroughs clearly articulated how this auxiliary would benefit the men and how a women's sector wasn't just necessary but invited by God. Her close relationship with L. G. Jordan was useful; because the auxiliary would directly assist the Foreign Missions, he aided in rallying votes.

The first WC had S. Willie Layton as president, Burroughs as corresponding secretary, Virginia Broughton as recording secretary, and Susie Foster as treasurer. "As corresponding secretary, 21-year-old Burroughs was responsible for gathering the activity reports from each state organization or society and compiling them into the annual report given at each convention. She also conducted the correspondence at the executive committee of the WC and was authorized to organize societies."[17] As a result, Burroughs built an abundance of relationships and worked to expand the reach of the organization. During her first year as secretary, Burroughs is said to have "labored 365 days, traveled 22,125 miles, delivered 215 speeches, organized a dozen societies, [written] 9,235 letters and received 4,820."[18] She was dedicated to the work and to making sure that the promises of efficacy she gave in her speech were true. Even though it was incredibly successful at creating opportunities for women and children and raising an abundance of money for the NBC, the Women's Convention was under the constant threat of being taken over by men. Burroughs fought to keep the WC separate. As much as the men wanted to downplay its efficacy, they couldn't deny the reality that the women were bringing in significant amounts of money that contributed extensively to the mission.

Burroughs's accomplishments through the WC are manifold, and I offer here a few highlights to show the range of her reach and her level of impact. By 1903, Burroughs reported that the organization represented a million Black Baptist women, which by 1904 included 480 new local societies and 102 children's bands. By 1920, the women had raised over $50,000 for missions—the equivalent of $1.5 million today.[19] Burroughs created several resources for mission training, including how to establish clubs and organizations on a local level, that were nationally pushed and promoted.[20] She also wrote and produced a play, *Slabtown District Convention: A Comedy in One Act*, which in a lot of ways was a satire of the WC.[21] Burroughs operated in many spheres, all with the goal of expanding of the reach of the work and of the WC.

In 1906, Burroughs established the first committee of her school, the National Training School for Women and Girls, which she would run out of the WC. She believed it was crucial for people, especially women and girls, to get training on the jobs they would be doing for their growth and safety. Reminiscing on not getting a teaching job out of high school, she said:

> An idea stuck out from the suffering of that disappointment that I would someday have a school here in Washington that school politics had nothing to do with, and that would give all sorts of girls a fair chance, without political pull, to help them overcome whatever handicaps they might have. It came to me like a flash of light, and I knew I was to do that thing (establish a school) when the time came. But I couldn't do it yet, so I just put the idea away in the back of my head and left it there.[22]

The initial version of the school was the Woman's Industrial Club, which she established when she first moved to Kentucky. This club addressed the needs of working women, providing "day and evening classes for the women in bookkeeping, shorthand, typing, sewing, cooking, child-care, hygiene, sanitation, cleaning and handicrafts."[23] The women paid ten cents for membership, made lunches to sell to Black workers, and purchased a house that provided a place for their activities as well as interim housing for people coming to work from other cities.

In 1901, Burroughs pitched the idea for the National Training School to the NBC and WC. She was unable to get support until 1904, and in 1906 they formed a school committee of eighty members from across the globe. Together they decided that Washington, DC, was the best site for the school because of the variety of people coming through town and the job possibilities there. Burroughs raised a lot of money and was able to establish a sustainable program, even though there were difficult moments financially. The school was funded through a myriad of resources:

> The school was funded by tuition and contributions from the WC, members of the Board of Trustees, Baptist churches, local churches of other denominations, women's missionary circles, individual donations and small financial gifts from White missionary societies and foundations. The school was supported primarily by Blacks and was never dependent on the support of Whites for its existence, unlike several other Black institutions.[24]

While the WC across the country raised money for the school, Burroughs also found private funding resources beyond institutional support because there was tension over what she was doing. For example, in 1938 the NBC voted to cut off financial support to the school because Burroughs refused to compromise her goals or adhere to any of their prescribed limitations of the Women's Convention. The NBC wanted to control the WC so that they would also control the finances, and she refused. The NBC then tried to vote her out at the 1939 convention, but the women stood up for themselves against their husbands and pastors, and she won the vote. Burroughs found enough funding that the school was out of debt by the time the NBC tried to reestablish relationship with the school, and Burroughs, years later.[25] She refused to let anything stop the progress of the work and her goals for opening the school.

Burroughs founded the National Training School for Women and Girls on principles that emerged from her work in the Women's Convention, which was grounded in a politics of respectability. As Evelyn Higginbotham asserts, "Through the discourse of respectability, the Baptist women emphasized manners and morals while simultaneously asserting traditional forms of protest, such as petitions, boycotts, and verbal appeals to justice. Ultimately: the rhetoric of the Woman's Convention combined both a conservative and a radical impulse."[26] The goal of the National Training School for Women and Girls was to educate and empower Black women and was called "the School of the Three Bs—the Holy Bible, the Bathtub, and the Broom. The Bible was a guide to everyday Christian living (Clean Lives), the Bathtub symbolized personal cleanliness (Clean Bodies), and the Broom symbolized cleanliness of the environment (Clean Homes)."[27] This aligned with Burroughs's focus on the principles of true womanhood, on which the school was founded. True womanhood prioritized ideals such as piety, modesty, domesticity, and uplifting the race as foundational.[28] Students were challenged to live with honor. In a letter to one of her students, Mary Dorsett, Burroughs writes, "Remember that you must always do your best and be your best because you are not only representing the race, but you are representing the womanhood of the race, and too many people expect the Negro women to be ordinary. It is a part of your business to be extraordinary."[29] This was the expectation to which she held her students and the esteem she had for them.

The school began with junior and high school divisions. Students could take sewing, dressmaking, housekeeping, and domestic sciences. It was a requirement for all students to take Black history, and the school hosted annual contests in Black historical essays and oratory.[30] Burroughs wanted to make sure that students knew their history and also felt proud to be learning and doing whatever they were engaged in. Access was also important. Students without the means to pay could work their way through school in the laundry facilities or receive other scholarships. Students would leave with a clear moral framework and skills to make a living, having had a top-quality education for wherever they were headed next.

Burroughs was active in many circles. In addition to her extensive work in the Women's Convention and her school, she was active in the NAACP, a founding member of the National League of Republican Colored Women, in several different women's clubs, and passionate about civil rights, women's suffrage, and the campaign against lynching.[31]

> Burroughs was very outspoken on the subject of women's suffrage. She worked hard for the passage of the 19th Amendment and denounced Black men who she felt had compromised the struggle for political equality. She said that, through cowardice or material gain, the men had misused the

vote. Burroughs urged her sisters to redeem the race through wise use of the ballot.[32]

Burroughs's involvement in broad networks helped her accomplish her goals. She worked alongside prominent others including Mary McLeod Bethune, Margaret Washington, Lugenia Hope, Mary Church Terrell, and Ida B. Wells-Barnett. Burroughs worked tirelessly to create support systems for Black women, which she saw as a vehicle to advance Black people as a whole. She believed that Black people could create a world in which they could not only survive, but one in which they could flourish—and that they didn't need help beyond themselves to accomplish it. This principle guided her life and work, and is clear in her proclaiming as well.

Introduction to the Artifacts

Burroughs's goal was to help Black people within religious and social institutions and beyond. Central to her rhetoric was her deep belief that she was called to serve God through *Christian service.* She believed that if Black women were supported, the rest of the race would be supported as well. Honor and virtue were paramount in her rhetoric, reflecting her grandmother's ideals. This contributed to the disdain Burroughs had for people who looked down on domestic workers because of their work, as if their value wasn't as high as others. An educator at heart, Burroughs used Bible verses to reinforce her ideas, and did so specifically to engage the dominant hearers in her audience, Black Christians, many of whom were also involved in various forms of Christian service. As Kelisha B. Graves argues, "A quick look at her archive reveals a woman who moved seamlessly between the gospel, education, and politics. She considered her work as a crusader for Christ to be her foremost call in the world."[33] Burroughs is special because she shows us that these areas that are often separated were deeply integrated for her. Her preaching wasn't specifically in the pulpit, although many of the spaces in which she operated were explicitly religious spaces. Addressing her audience through text and theological nuance, she found language that exhibited political prowess in order to articulate what should be done in the name of God—specifically, that women should be able to contribute.

The remainder of this chapter will examine two moments from the early years of Burroughs's proclaiming journey that show the foundation that she continued to stand on for years after. I will look at "How the Sisters Are Hindered from Helping" and "The Colored Woman and Her Relation to the Domestic Problem."[34] The first speech is foundational to Burroughs's work on behalf of Black women and her deep desire for them to have their own spaces to flourish—acknowledging that this aim is often hindered by the power of men in those spheres. Her speaking focuses on evoking action and asserting new ways of being. The second speech announces her disdain for the contempt of workers. These two homiletical artifacts offer critical lenses into Burroughs's preaching rhetoric as a whole.

Background

"How the Sisters Are Hindered from Helping" (hereafter "How the Sisters") was Nannie Helen Burroughs's first public proclamation and one of the moments for which she is most known.[35] She offered this address at the National Baptist Convention in 1900 as a precursor to the vote over whether women would be able to have their own sphere of influence as the Women's Convention. Although the specific reason she was asked to speak is uncertain, it is safe to assume that she may have been a delegate from her church, and/or that her connection with Jordan (in Foreign Missions) gave her more widespread renown. Regardless, "to be a convention speaker, one had to be well known in Black Baptist circles. [Her friend] Harrison points out that Burroughs was in great demand to speak at church gatherings."[36] This was when Burroughs moved from more administrative positions to the forefront, advocating for Black women to have a proper place in the work of the church, and specifically in the NBC. This particular moment of proclaiming was intended to help the Women's

Convention initiative move forward in establishing a women's auxiliary. It had been tried before but denied for several years. After Burroughs's speech, however, the vote passed, and the Women's Convention was established in that same convention.

"The Colored Woman and Her Relation to the Domestic Problem" (hereafter "The Domestic Problem") was Burroughs's proclamation at the Negro Young People's Christian Congress held in 1902.[37] She was one of many speakers, but her address garnered significant notoriety. A report from the event stated:

> The distinctive feature of last night's session of the negro congress was the address made by a younger woman, Nannie H. Burroughs, of Washington, D.C., on the subject "The Colored Woman and Her Relation to the Domestic Problem." The power of clear, close thinking and the ability to give expression to her wholesome thoughts and sound advice in the choicest and clearest language was received with surprise, but with marked appreciation, by the immense throng gathered in the auditorium, among the audience being a number of white people. She made a strong plea for the recognition of the dignity of labor by the women of the race and maintained that the "race problem" would be largely solved when the salvation of the negro woman was assured. At the conclusion of her address a large number of those present, among them several white people, went to her and personally thanked her for the timely words of wisdom which she had spoken.[38]

Among the various speakers, including Booker T. Washington, in different formats and locations at this meeting, Burroughs's speech was revered as one of the most dynamic and impactful moments of the entire session.[39] She wanted Black people to be able to compete in the industrial world of the time. If Black people, especially Black women, were not competent for the jobs allotted, they would be unemployed and unable to care for themselves.[40] Burroughs's aim was to explain why it was important to train Black women and why it was equally critical not to demean work and discredit the honor of the domestic worker.

Homiletical Insights

A Clear Problem and a Clear Solution

Burroughs didn't have the luxury of abstract illustrations or rhetoric unsupported by clear pragmatic ends. Everything she spoke was for the purpose of immediate action from her audience, consistently for a cause that would help Black people. She asked clear questions and offered clearer answers, so that after she spoke her hearers would know *exactly* what was being asked of them. As a preacher outside of the pulpit, her rhetoric was rooted in a particular cause that was more specific than a general gospel message. The clarity of her rhetoric, in addition to the passion with which she spoke, made for compelling messages that often got her asked back. More importantly, what she advocated for often came to pass, as we see with the vote over the Women's Convention and the building of the training school.

In addition, the itinerancy of non-pulpit preaching—even if there were repeated hearers in the crowd—didn't leave room for Burroughs to depend upon a foundation laid by previous messages. She had to say what she meant in the moment, because it might be the only time her audience would hear her speak. She capitalized on the moment with clarity of purpose, including how she asked people to respond to what she was saying. I begin my catalog of her homiletical strategies here because her positionality as activist-educator alongside preacher-proclaimer, coupled with life experiences that showed her why advocating for Black women was so critical, creates a different type of urgency for her rhetoric.

In "How the Sisters," Burroughs asks directly, "Will you as a pastor and friend of missions help by not hindering these women when they come among you to speak and to enlist the women of your church?"[41] She is not asking for the hearers' assistance in the work, nor is she asking that they exert specific energy to produce something for the women. Burroughs is merely asking that they commit to not getting in the way of the women and not hindering their ability to do the work they are called to do.

Women are seeking to be helpful, and the men are simply asked not to stand in their way. The entire artifact is built on invoking a response—noninterference—to this question.

Burroughs argues that the lack of hindrance by men (as opposed to their active help) is itself important and asserts the positive impact that this "lack" of action will have. Her aim was to get them to vote for the separate auxiliary of the Women's Convention. The message needed to be clear so that when it was time to vote the substantive reasons behind the choice could be understood from her rhetoric: Women should be allowed to be helpful, and men are simply asked not to get in their way.

Burroughs's rhetoric in "The Domestic Problem" is equally clear. Her underlying concern is that educated Black people were looking down on Black women who were domestic workers and not recognizing how critical they were to helping the race at large. The solution was a change in behavior and outlook, such that domestic work would be seen through the lens of honor, and training would be widely provided. Burroughs argues, "The training of Negro women is absolutely necessary, not only for their own salvation and the salvation of the race, but because the hour in which we live demands it. If we lose sight of the demands of the hour, we blight our hope to progress."[42] This critical quote, which is spoken early and reiterated throughout, makes clear the foundation of her message, even without hearing the rest of the proclamation.[43]

The Sacred Self: The Salvific Ends of Black Women's Presence and Participation

One of the grounding rhetorical threads of Burroughs's preaching is the salvific nature of Black women's presence and participation. She repeatedly speaks about the salvific nature of Black women's work and the ways that Black women can provide the solution to issues if the hearers will simply support (and/or not hinder) what they are aiming to do. While she does not often use personal narrative, she refers to Black women consistently, which includes her. Black men are also supported by these efforts, as they will both have help and avoid getting in the way of what God has called the women to do, and the world at large is saved for a variety of reasons. Burroughs's explicit use of "salvation," as opposed to "help" or another non-religious term, points to a larger, eschatological reality towards which she is aiming and within which she locates her work theologically. She aligns the elevation of Black women and their work with the telos of salvation in the gospel narrative in a way that would have been commonly known in Black religious spaces. For Burroughs, the tasks of service, work, excellence, and honor aren't merely "good human" things, but are all things for the glory of God—and Black women have the capacity to carry out the honor and service that God desires. This is foundational in her rhetoric and critical for understanding her as a preacher in the early twentieth century. This would be an important message at any time, but in the early twentieth century Black men were focused on the "race problem" and the salvific liberating telos of civil rights, and assumed that a "gender problem" and the saving work of women's rights was not something that required discussion. As such, Burroughs makes clear that her voice is not for the general public; she is specifically naming and advocating theologically and eschatologically for Black women—which for her is where advocating for Black life must begin.

In "How the Sisters," Burroughs explicitly names Black women's service and help as a solution. She takes those who were seen as "helpmates" to Black men—Black women—and elevates them as the solution in their own right. She posits, "For a number of years there has been a righteous discontent, a burning zeal to go forward in his name among the Baptist women of our churches and it will be the dynamic force in the religious campaign at the opening of the 20th century. It will be the spark that shall light the altar fire in the heathen lands."[44] This "altar fire in the heathen lands" was an illustration of the presence of God in the places where God's light was not seen as prevalent. Because the work she was asking to do had a missional end, her aim was to argue that when Black women serve, they bring the light of God where the light has not been.[45]

She continues, "We come now to the rescue. We unfurl our banner upon which is inscribed this motto, 'The World for Christ. Woman, Arise, He calleth for Thee.'"[46] She states that the men "toil unceasingly" and supports her claim of rescue (giving it salvific undertones) by declaring that this is not just something that the women have thought of, but that Jesus is calling them to this work, and it will change lives—including the lives of those have tried to get in their way (the Baptist men).[47] Her strategic framing makes it clear that Black women's work will save the world and will rescue the men, but she also addresses the organization by claiming the work will secure more funding, and the mission will benefit and be saved as well.

Along with the solution and rescue aspects, Burroughs also names the consequences of inaction: "We realize to allow these gems to lie unpolished longer means a loss to the denomination."[48] The organization doesn't just maintain its status quo but suffers a loss by not allowing these women to do their work; the women will save the men from labor and failure and spark excellent fire in new areas. The organization needs the women. Burroughs closes with very practical information and financial numbers indicating the impact of the help and the pragmatic ramifications of women's work. This is the grounding presence of this sermon. Black women are the answer and are ready to come to the rescue. Her invitation is, simply: Do not get in the way of such necessary work.

In "The Domestic Problem," Burroughs posits her strategy for creating better training for Black women and lifts up the labor of the domestic worker as salvific for Black women and therefore salvific for the Black race. Like in the previous artifact, she uses language like "rescue" to describe how Black women's work affects the whole. In the opening of her sermon, she says,

> May I venture forward in this hour to make a plea for a class of women of my race whose number is legion? May I plead for the moral and industrial salvation of two-thirds of the women of this country, women who by the sweat of their brow must eat bread? I refer to the honest working woman. If this class of women arise, they will push forward, higher

> and higher, the principles espoused by negro women who are laboring for the salvation of the masses. If they fall, they will pull down with them, for it is impossible for us to rise unless we take the masses of our sisters with us.[49]

In this opening invitation, she situates Black women's well-being as that which literally saves the rest of the race. This piece is important because it suggests salvation as both a "saving for" in relation to the domestic workers for whom she's advocating, and a "saving from" in the sense of the moral salvation of those who look down on them. Broadly, this salvation benefits the whole Black community. After setting up what she calls "the domestic problem," she says, "The solution of this problem will be the prime factor in the salvation of Negro womanhood, whose salvation must be attained before the so-called race problem can be solved." Black women are prioritized, but *lifting up* Black women—specifically those women who have been seen as "less than" and/or as not holding a particular type of honor—is indeed the needed salvation.

Anticipatory Reading of Rhetorical Context

Nannie H. Burroughs was known to speak often and to large groups of people. She frequently spoke to Christian groups, to activist organizations, and at larger conferences, and the diversity of hearers shifted from context to context. Her attentiveness to the specificity of context as a basis for shaping her rhetoric is a critical homiletical insight. In any context, her rhetoric was almost exclusively aimed at the Black people in the room. However, her attention to context also reminds us of the diversity of Black folks. Much of her speaking was to the girls at her school, the assembly of the National Baptist Convention, or in other political or educational spheres where most Black people present were educated. These were all very different contexts. Therefore, the use of particular rhetorical strategies specific to each context elevates her as a rhetor and an effective preacher.

In these artifacts, Burroughs uses these strategies in two ways: (1) anticipating *backlash* and addressing it (preemptive anticipation), and (2) anticipating specific understandings of honor in order to challenge them (corrective anticipation). These were geared towards the population to whom she was speaking, and while they may have had a broader impact on the people who later read the manuscripts, we can see their immediate effect through the responsive actions of the hearers. Knowing your audience and how they might receive you is critical for Black women; we often enter spaces where hearers have already decided who we are and what we do or do not bring to the table.

In "How the Sisters," Burroughs does a masterful job anticipating backlash by framing her proclamation with words intentionally aimed to put hearers at ease and enable them to then hear her straightforward question. Her audience was Black men of the NBC, many of whom had already voted against the very thing for which she was advocating, specifically because they did not want to use their resources to create a space that they could not control. Knowing these things, she says, "We come not to usurp thrones nor to sow discord, but to so organize and systematize the work that each church may help through a Woman's Missionary society and not be made poorer thereby."[50] "We" refers to the women, and essentially, she is saying that they aren't trying to take over the men's space, which had been a part of the pushback. She says, "We realize that to allow these gems to lie unpolished longer means a loss to the denomination."[51] Men wanted their "helpmates" to be just that and not have their own spheres of influence, lest they take over in some form or fashion. Burroughs is saying that a takeover is not the aim, articulating what they were *not* there to do as a way to open up what they *were* going to do—which was to offer help through their own ways to the entire denomination. She recognized that as a young Black woman in this Baptist environment, she was already seen as a subversive presence. She was likely to put folks on edge such that her message would be unable to be heard. So, she names this problem in hopes of consoling the egos of the audience in order to actually be heard.

Similarly, in "The Domestic Problem," Burroughs uses the specificity of the context to shape her rhetorical push. She isn't anticipating backlash as much as a tension between established perspectives of honor and virtue and the plea that she is making. Whereas in "How the Sisters" she aims to soften the message, in "The Domestic Problem" Burroughs uses the notions of honor and virtue, which were consistent themes throughout the conference, to enliven and thrust forward her rhetoric. She takes time to outline why normative understandings are problematic and dangerous for the flourishing of Black women and the race at large, and she publicly scorns those who would attack the women she would support. Burroughs argues, "When the nobility of labor is magnified, and those who do labor are respected more because of their real worth to the race, we will find less number trying to escape the brand, 'servant girl.' We are not less honorable if we are servants."[52] She is inviting the educated people to whom she is speaking to see honor and virtue in positions that have been seen as dishonorable. Burroughs argues, "The race whose women have not learned that industry and self-respect are the only guarantees of a true character will find itself bound by ignorance and violence or fettered with chains of poverty."[53] Again, using honor and character as her basis because of their frequency in this particular conference, she pushes the notion and identifies that what some have deemed dishonorable is not. She was angry at people who would mock the domestic worker, especially since she saw them as foundational to the race. With remarks like, "Fidelity to duty rather than the grade of one's occupation is the true measure of character," and "Industry is one of the noblest virtues of any race. The people who scorn and frown upon her must die," she argues that honor and virtue are found in those whom some in the crowd might consider the least honorable, which is something that needs to change.[54]

Interpreting Texts: Scripture and God Talk as Sources of Authority

In both artifacts, Burroughs uses scriptural references as a form of historical and anecdotal memory for those listening. The use of Scripture in "How the Sisters" is intriguing because it is not primarily exegetical but used in a way that is explicitly designed to lend legitimation and authority to her ideas. For instance, Burroughs says, "It has ever been from the time of Miriam, the most remarkable woman, the sister of Moses, the most remarkable man, down to the courageous women that in very recent years have carried the Gospel into Tibet and Africa and proclaimed and taught the truth where no man has been allowed to enter."[55] Burroughs pairs Miriam and Moses. That Moses's character was remarkable would have been commonly understood. However, Miriam was not as frequently discussed, and Burroughs positions her directly next to Moses. Burroughs's claim that Miriam is equally as "remarkable" as Moses, and pairing her with the women carrying the gospel in more recent times, writes in Miriam as a historical precedent for women doing the work of God today. By bringing in Miriam, Burroughs reminds her audience that the biblical men they love so much have had women doing the work alongside them. She knows how to speak to this audience and how to operate in this space—but she is also just telling the truth. Burroughs closes this paragraph by saying, "Surely, women somehow have had a very important part in the work saving this redeemed earth."[56] This just feels like it has a hint of sarcasm to it, which is not uncommon for Burroughs as she was known to use wit as a rhetorical strategy. Alongside expanding memory, there is some play involved. She uses biblical characters to remind those listening that what she is asking for is not unfounded but biblical. In this case the Bible is not the center of her rhetoric but referential as a common source of authority for this group of hearers.

Similarly, in "The Domestic Problem," Burroughs uses scriptural references as familiar touchpoints of illustration. In one, she uses John the Baptist to name the preposterous things that women would rather do than be seen as a servant, even though domestic work is an honor, not a deficit. After calling such women "parlor ornaments," she says, "These are women at service who would eat their meals off the heads of barrels or dress after the fashion of John the Baptist in the wilderness before they would sacrifice their high-toned moral character, simply to shine in the social world by virtue of their idleness and ability to dress well."[57] Again, John the Baptist and his wild appearance were known by the audience, so she was able to reference them as a way to lend authority to her message. Her other scriptural allusion is in talking about why being a servant is just a part of being a human. She argues, "God made us all servants the very day he dismissed Adam from Eden. . . . 'By the sweat of thy brow shalt thou eat bread.' What mean these women who are eating bread and not sweating, either, by scorning the women who are obeying the divine injunction?"[58] It is no coincidence that she named Adam, because her point is that we were all made to work. And these women are, as she puts it, simply "following the divine injunction." So why are we aiming to dishonor their clearly honorable work?

Finally, in "The Domestic Problem," Burroughs cleverly draws in God to talk about how Black people are perceived, and to argue that whether or not it is true, it simply shows how far God can bring them:

> They tell us we came from apes and baboons, and we have made it this far. Further, if God could take a crop of apes or baboons and make beings like us He is God indeed, and we can trust him to raise us from servants to queens. If we did come from these ungainly animals of the four-footed family, we got here nearly as soon as the people who didn't have so far to come.[59]

In this moment, she aims to say it doesn't matter where we come from or who says where we are coming from; God can and will elevate us to royalty. She is also aiming to say, don't let white people (the "they" in her sentence) convince us that this work is not honorable because of who they have told us that we are. She uses God language to legitimate her message and remind the hearer that honor and greatness can come from humble beginnings, no matter one's origin story (again, without necessarily agreeing with what "they" said). She aligns salvific and God-like participation with a type of societal stability. We *can* win. So how do we win? We stop thinking that being a domestic worker is bad—and even if we do, we remember that *God* deems places honorable regardless of a societal norm that would articulate otherwise.

Conclusion

Nannie Helen Burroughs was a dynamic preacher who saw her work as creating space and opportunity for Black women, who had often been disregarded, to be supported and seen. She offered an incredibly textured witness to the times in which she lived and the spheres in which she operated. The fruit of all she did spoke for itself. She created jobs, opportunities, and schools and pushed those with power to help to create tangible progress as well. Her upbringing alongside her mother, who fought for her place as a domestic worker, and her brief time also as a domestic worker when she was unable to get a job as a teacher, deeply informed the work that she sought. Her embodiment as a Black woman gave her insight into the peculiar situation of Black women within the Black community and the American context generally. Her advocacy stemmed from her knowledge and her sense of urgency, requiring a response from those who heard her.

Nannie Helen Burroughs believed to her core that there were practices to move Black people in the direction of being self-sustaining, strong, and well. As a preacher, she shows us how her story and her praxis, rooted in ministry as a practice of life and in the everyday struggles of being a Black woman in the twentieth century, deeply informed how she preached and advocated for the good news of Black flourishing. Burroughs's rhetorical witness spanned institutions and platforms that didn't always directly overlap. From her, we are reminded of the clarity needed when one requires a specific response. We gain access to what salvation in the here and now that is inspired and led by Black women looks like through her eyes. She invites us to consider more deeply what it means to use Scripture as a familiar authoritative lens that includes Black women, beyond a particular type of exposition, and she encourages us to consider the necessity of deeply contextual language for purposes that can be both preemptive and corrective in relation to hegemonic reactions and interpretations.

Burroughs invites us to consider the necessity of response to the preaching moment and the actual telos of preaching. When we consider her proclamation in the canon of preachers, we see her style of preaching conveys that preaching should evoke action. For her, the necessary response was action, movement, and progress for Black people in tangible ways that could be seen and quantified. Preaching was not about the symbolic "thoughts and prayers," but about changing policies, enacting votes, and moving Black people forward in a way that could be qualitatively and concretely identified. This type of preaching is not only intended to change the hearts of the hearers, but to inspire a new way of living that has critical effects on the community in which they operate. She believed in Black people and in destigmatizing different spheres in which Black women operated, such that they would be acknowledged and treated as the critically important people they were. Her preaching set a precedent for her practice in bringing schools and opportunities into existence that would make this elevation possible. As she said, "It is not the depths from which we come but the heights to which we soar."[60]

4
Too Sick to Be Silent, Too Tired Not to Talk
The Life and Preaching Practice of Fannie Lou Hamer

"I am sick and tired of being sick and tired."[1]

"We have to build our own power. We have to win every single political office we can, where we have a majority of Black people. . . . Just because this cracker is starting to show us a few teeth and talk nice doesn't mean he'll move over and let us have some of that power."[2] Fannie Lou Hamer was an activist, a community organizer, and a woman in relentless pursuit of rights for Black people in the United States. She believed that Black people could and should be able to participate fully in the political sphere as a means of creating access to the rights and addressing the needs Black people had. Hamer knew that the conditions Black people suffered were not only unacceptable, but that they could and must be changed. A native Mississippian, she experienced firsthand the violence and injustice present in Mississippi and specifically advocated for those in Mississippi whose voices had been left out of conversations on justice.

Although her witness in the civil rights movement is celebrated now, there were mixed opinions about her presence and rhetorical ability because of her speaking style, which reflected her particular location as a poor Black woman in the Mississippi Delta. In addition to racism, she encountered sexism, classism, and fatphobia as the fullness of her embodiment pushed against both whiteness and performances of Black respectability. Regardless, there is no denying that Fannie Lou Hamer's voice was critical in revealing the conditions of Mississippi and proclaiming that God was not pleased and would not stand with the America that operated in such hateful ways. As a proclaimer, Hamer was known for integrating singing, often of hymns, into her speaking and moving crowds with her voice, her testimony, and her practical application of biblical stories. She was known widely as an activist and orator, and here we will listen to her as a preacher.

Hamer's proclamation was a direct response to the dire situation into which she was born, and which she refused to consider the final word for herself and other Black people. There is no place in America untouched by the prevalence and violence of racism, and the Mississippi Delta was known to be one of the more egregiously violent and horrific areas for Black people to live. Hamer recounts several personal stories of police brutality, unwarranted arrest, and terror at the hands of white mobs of "cowards," as she would often refer to them.[3] While her public witness did not begin until she was in her forties, the fodder for her proclamation came from a lifetime of witnessing injustice against and the demeaning of Black people—yet being told by her mother that she should be proud to be Black. She lived her life believing what her mother said and fighting for Black people to be able to participate in the world as equally as their white counterparts.

To study Fannie Lou Hamer's life is to understand the pillars that were foundational to her preaching ministry. Her witness shows preaching in the sphere of community organizing, undergirded by Christian rhetoric but resistant to any faith that would speak without acting. Three of the homiletical insights unique to her are: (1) storytelling as a strategy of truth, (2) the constant use of *we* to proclaim collective responsibility, and (3) Scripture as moral foundation. We can excavate these from her preaching ministry at large and specifically through two artifacts: "We're on Our Way," from the beginning of her public ministry in 1964, and "We Haven't

Arrived Yet," which emerged towards the end of her life in 1976. Who Fannie Lou Hamer was is clearly displayed in what she said, and her particularity in turn offers rich contributions to homiletics.

Her-Story: Fannie Lou Hamer

Fannie Lou Hamer (née Townsend) was born in Mississippi on October 6, 1917, the youngest of Jim and Ella Townsend's twenty children. Both of her parents were sharecroppers, but her father was also a Baptist preacher and a "bootlegger" in the community, and her mother was a domestic worker in white homes.[4] When discussing her childhood, Hamer talked about the difficulties of growing up poor, but because of the principles that her mother instilled in her, she spoke with pride. Thinking back, Hamer said, "My mother was a great woman. She went through a lot of suffering to bring the twenty of us up, but she still taught us to be decent and to respect ourselves, and that is one of the things that has kept me going."[5] In one instance, the young Fannie Lou Hamer decided she wanted to be white. As a child she looked around and saw that white people had all of the things that she wanted—proper food, clothing, access—so she decided that she wanted to be white. Hamer recalls Ella Townsend saying, "'I don't ever want to hear you say that again, honey!' She said, 'you respect yourself as a little child, a little black child. And as you grow older, respect yourself as a black woman. Then one day, other people will respect you.'"[6] Her mother's wisdom was a major influence throughout Hamer's life, stemming from this moment when she was a child. We see this wisdom echoed in her rhetoric: being proud to be Black, fighting to have equitable rights as Black woman, and moving through the world with respect and honor for oneself.

Family greatly shaped Hamer's story and experiences. The Townsend family was very poor, which was common for a Black family in Mississippi, and Hamer knew poverty intimately. She recounts, "So many times for dinner we would have greens with no seasoning and flour gravy."[7] At times they went without shoes: "We wouldn't have on shoes or anything because we didn't have them. She [Ella Townsend] would always tie our feet up with rags because the ground would be froze real hard."[8] Sometimes a plantation owner would tell Hamer's mother that they could gather the scraps of crops in a field, but to do so they would have to walk barefoot to get what they could. Her mother would also help white families kill hogs, and the families would then give her the intestines, feet, and head.[9] At one point, the Townsend family started to get on their feet and stopped sharecropping in order to build on their own land. They had a house for themselves and cattle that would secure a future for the family. When they were gone one evening, some white men from the community came and poisoned their cattle. They returned to see that their piece of financial hope was gone, which made it almost impossible for them to get out of poverty again. They had to go back to sharecropping in order to make ends meet.[10]

Most Black people in that time and place were sharecroppers, and Black children were not left out of that work. One anecdote Hamer often mentioned as an eye-opening and painful moment in her own life occurred when she was six years old and was manipulated by a white plantation owner to pick cotton for some food and treats. He offered her food in exchange for work, which created an agreement no six-year-old would understand. She accepted the treats, went, and worked—only to realize that this exchange would keep her tied to this plantation owner. In the end, she would be picking hundreds of pounds of cotton each day while only earning one dollar for it.[11] This was not an uncommon practice in the area where she grew up. Anger over such exploitation of even children shows up in her passionate testimony and advocacy for freedom and for "Black self-reliance"[12]

Needing to sharecrop for survival, Hamer was unable to go to school beyond sixth grade. Although she wasn't given a lot of schooling, she loved school when she was able to go. The Black schools in Mississippi were desperately underfunded, and Black students were only in school from December to March because of the sharecropping season. Hamer was a bright student, winning spelling bees and other oratorical competitions. After sixth grade, supporting her family had to be her priority.[13] She heeded her mother's words of wisdom, however: Learn to read because "when you read, you know—and you can help yourself and others."[14] This wisdom and these experiences were in the marrow of her bones as an adult and came forth through her rhetoric as well.

Faith was also a critical thread in Fannie Lou Hamer's life. At twelve she joined Home Baptist Church and was baptized in the Quiver River in Sumner, Mississippi. As she grew older, she could quote the Bible better than most people, which she demonstrated with skill in her sermons, especially considering that they were extemporaneous. She began to interrogate and question how churches were operating in response to the depth of injustice taking place around them. This questioning and wondering shows up repeatedly in her public rhetoric, alongside her deep reliance on faith and biblical stories. For Hamer, faith was critical: "'Christianity should be being concerned about your fellow man, not building a million-dollar church while people are starving around the corner,' Mrs. Hamer said. 'Christ was a revolutionary, out there where it was happening. That's what God is all about, and that's where I get my strength.'"[15] That strength would carry her through the most excruciating moments of her life.

In 1944, when she was twenty-seven years old, Fannie Lou Townsend met and fell in love with Pap Hamer, to whom she stayed married throughout her life. They had difficulties having biological children but eventually adopted: "By 1954, the Hamers had begun caring for two young girls that they adopted: nine-year-old Dorothy Jean, the offspring of a single mother unable to care for her, and five-month-old Virgie Ree, a burn victim whose parents were too poor to provide adequate medical care."[16]

During this time, the Hamers lived and worked on the Marlow plantation in Ruleville, Mississippi. In addition to ongoing white violence carried out against Black people in Montgomery County, Hamer also experienced personal violence at the hands of a doctor in 1961. Hamer was scheduled to have an ovarian cyst removed, but was instead given a hysterectomy. Writing about this incident, Kay Mills says of Hamer, “There was one more crucial element that molded a poor sharecropper into a leader: it was anger, touched with sorrow about her lack of control over her own life. Without her knowledge or permission, Fannie Lou Hamer was sterilized in 1961.”[17] Medical malpractice, especially sterilization, against Black women was not unusual and had actually grown to be a common occurrence in Mississippi—another injustice that had to be fought.

The following year, civil rights workers from the Student Nonviolent Coordinating Committee (SNCC) came to Ruleville and held a mass gathering to try to get Black people registered to vote, a seemingly impossible task in Mississippi. Hamer’s anger at the unjust circumstances of her life and her complete unwillingness to accept such circumstances as the continued reality for Black people became the fuel for her response. Although she initially had not planned on going to the SNCC meeting, her attendance became a major turning point in her life. From that point on, she became actively and loudly involved in advocacy for voting rights.

This was the beginning of the Fannie Lou Hamer who became known publicly—starting when she raised her hand to say she would go register to vote. In reflecting on the gathering, Hamer noted, “Until then I’d never heard of no mass meeting and I didn’t know that a Negro could register and vote.”[18] But during the meeting, she not only encouraged others to try to vote, she used her role as a community leader (she was a timekeeper on a plantation) and her testimony to remind those present what they were up against. As June Jordan said, “Her bravery made them brave.”[19] The summer of 1962 marked Hamer’s formal entry into the civil rights movement. Arrests, bombings, and job dismissals followed, but Hamer continued working as a field secretary with the SNCC during the early 1960s. She conducted door-to-door canvassing and taught citizenship classes throughout the rural South.[20]

Registering to Vote

By the early 1960s, Mississippi had made it almost impossible for Black people to vote. One tactic was to require registrants to pass difficult literacy tests focused on obscure parts of the Mississippi State Constitution. White men would also show up with guns, attempting to intimidate Black voters and incite fear as they registered one by one. After one group of Black people was unable to register in Indianola and was heading home, their rented bus got stopped for being the wrong color. A yellow bus was, of course, a standard color, so the charge that it was the "wrong color" was simply a way to issue a fine for driving while Black. According to Susan Kling, this incident was a significant turning point in Hamer's personal fight against racism: "Beginning with the Indianola experience, Hamer moved from being an individual whose sole means of 'resistance' was survival to being one who took initiatives to promote collective struggle for real power. As she began resisting on a different level during her SNCC years and after, the stakes and positive consequences grew in direct proportion."[21]

Hamer didn't let this first "no" stop her, and she went back again to register—and this time succeeded. However, as a result of registering, Hamer lost her job. The owner of the Marlow plantation, where she was working, told her that she would have to recall her registration form if she wanted to work there. Hamer's final response was, "Mr. Dee, I didn't go down there to register for you. I went there to register for myself."[22] After having to leave the plantation—and her family—she, alongside other activists, became a target of violence. On September 10, 1963, ten days after her eviction from the plantation, sixteen bullets were fired into the Tucker home, where she was staying, fortunately missing all human targets.[23] Terror and fear-based intimidation from white locals ensued, including from white local police officers trying to shut down the activists and make Hamer pay for helping them register to vote.

Winona

Fannie Lou Hamer continued to advocate for voter registration, literacy, and economic freedom despite the threats against herself and her family. There was a high cost. One of the most frequent testimonies that became foundational to her preaching—and was the catalyst for her public and national witness because she gave it on national television—came from a horrific and terror-filled experience in Winona, Mississippi, on June 9, 1963. On a bus ride back from a training about literacy, Hamer and her seven coworkers stopped at a bus stop. A few of them went in and demanded to be served at the counter. They were harassed by police officers and decided to leave. They went back outside, and as was customary they began to collect information on their assailants (license plate, names, etc.) before getting back on the bus. The white officers inside got wind of this from a white man who had been observing outside. Hamer, who was one of the oldest on the trip, got off the bus to see what was happening and was told by her companions, who were being arrested, to get back on. As she was getting back on the bus, the officers demanded her arrest as well. Once she was inside the police car, they kicked her and harassed her all the way to Montgomery County jail. All who were taken into custody were beaten along the way and told repeatedly they were going to be taught a lesson. At the prison, they were put into single cells and received brutal, individual beatings. June Johnson was the first to be beaten, and they could all hear her screaming. Johnson had irreparable damage to her eye and a permanent knot on her head. Each of their accounts reflected this type of brutality.

After calling to Ruleville and confirming her reputation as a voter registration worker, officers came to Hamer's cell and told her she was going to wish she were dead.[24] Hamer recounts, "They put me in a cell with these two Negro prisoners and threatened them if they didn't beat me. They gave one of the men a long blackjack and made him beat me till he was exhausted. Then, when he was tired, the second one sat on my feet and beat me some more. They beat me till my body was hard, till I couldn't bend my fingers or get up when they told me to. That's how I got this blood clot in my left eye—the sight's nearly gone now. And my kidney was injured from the blows they gave me in the back."[25] The attack was also sexualized, as they pulled her dress up as she kept trying to pull it down. She fought back and was threatened that the beating would become even more severe if she continued to resist. After she was beaten, she continued to hear the other young women crying out in pain as well.[26] The group was detained for four days, suffering under conditions of not being fed, being burned in the showers with scalding water, and intimately witnessing one another's excruciating beatings. After their trial, they were forced at gunpoint to sign statements that said they had beaten each other.[27] It took the combined efforts of the SNCC, the Southern Christian Leadership Conference, and a petition to Martin Luther King Jr. for the group to be released. All of this was needed to get six people released from jail based on unfounded charges—for simply daring to claim their rights as Black people.

After their release from jail, Hamer was taken to a hospital in Atlanta because of the severity of her injuries. She did not let her family or her husband visit because she did not want them to see her "in such bad shape."[28] Hamer remarked, "I just wonder how many more times is America gonna turn its head and pretend nothin' is happening. I used to think the Justice Department was just what it said—justice. I asked one of those men, 'Have y'all got a Justice Department or an Injustice Department?'"[29] Winona represented one of the most painful tragedies of Hamer's life. Even with the trauma lingering in her body, she would later use this story on state and national stages as concrete evidence of the experience of Black people in Mississippi. She didn't shy away from the details because it was critical to her that people knew the truth of that harrowing experience. This story and other narratives of oppression and cruelty are central to Hamer's rhetorical witness.

To the National Stage: The 1964 Democratic National Convention

On April 26, 1964, Fannie Lou Hamer and a few hundred other Mississippians went to the Democratic National Convention to form the Mississippi Freedom Democratic Party (MFDP) as a response to the all-white delegation that did not represent the population of Mississippi. By this time, Hamer was well known throughout Mississippi as an activist fighting voter suppression and economic disparity. However, after the DNC she achieved national notoriety. During the appeal for the Freedom Democratic Party, Hamer gave a testimony of what happened to her in the Winona jail. "By the end of her eight minutes, Hamer had exposed Mississippi for the sadistic brutality so characteristic of its treatment of blacks. Filled with emotion, Hamer wept. 'I felt just like I was telling it from the mountain,' she told a *Jet* reporter, Larry Still. 'That's why I like that song "Go tell it on the mount." I feel like I'm talking to the world.'"[30] Although the television network quickly cut away from Hamer's testimony to cover a press conference held by President Johnson, in order to lessen the impact of her statement, the MFDP received hundreds of telegrams in support of its efforts. In addition, the MFDP was offered a compromise of two seats, which Hamer adamantly demanded that they should not take—much to the dismay of leaders like Martin Luther King Jr. who believed they should start with a compromise. For her, the audacity of a compromise was a slap in the face to those who were demanding freedom and an equal voice that was representative of the population of Mississippi. She made vocally clear that she would not accept two seats at the convention, and the party sided with her.[31]

From this point on, Hamer found herself on the national stage, weaving testimony with biblical admonitions for America to be more just for Black people. Her repeated assertion that America was "sick" and needed to get better and do better became a consistent theme throughout her messaging, alongside clear biblical support for the claims she was making. In addition to speaking, "Hamer began concentrating her efforts on economic self-reliance through the Mississippi Freedom Labor Union, Head Start programs, and the Freedom Farm Corporation, a cooperative venture she established to feed, clothe, and house Mississippi's poor. In many ways, the building of the corporation was largely a one-woman effort."[32] She raised money and inspired people in surrounding areas to create similar programs. Although she wasn't always respected by middle-class civil rights leaders because of how her speech patterns portrayed her lack of education, nobody could deny her impact. She was more concerned with seeing the manifestations of Black survival and care, then performing a typing of Black respectability that would make her palatable to those who had critiques.

Fannie Lou Hamer suffered the consequences of daring to be a Black woman who believed in her freedom in a world of white supremacy and racism. Her husband was often fired from his jobs as a direct result of her advocacy and the work they were doing out of their home to help feed and collect food for others. They repeatedly suffered police harassment and had a myriad of threats aimed at them. Hamer spent her life sharing all she had with others, building systems of mutual aid in Black communities, and proclaiming about the realities of Mississippi—adding her unique voice to the movement for Black freedom. On March 14, 1977, Fannie Lou Hamer died of cancer. Her tombstone in Ruleville includes her famous quote, "I am sick and tired of being sick and tired."

Introduction to the Artifacts: The Voice of the Mississippi Delta

Fannie Lou Hamer's preaching was a response to her own experience, rooted in the urgency of the times. After the 1962 Ruleville meeting, she spent a great deal of time speaking across different platforms and inviting people into the change that she wanted to see. Her extemporaneous style was woven with narrative, and she advocated for a justice that included poor, Black Mississippi Delta residents, of which she was one. Her rhetoric was a product of her practice, seen through her storytelling, her immense knowledge of the Bible, and current events that she threads together in her invitations to others to join the work. This was hard work, and she knew it. She spoke testimony interwoven with biblical instruction, advocating for real change and critiquing any rhetoric and practice (especially from pastors) that offered no practical implications. Hamer wasn't asking people to do something that she was not actively participating in herself. She put her own body and life on the line for a cause she felt was worthy of the sacrifice:

championing the freedom of Black people, particularly by increasing their economic prosperity and fighting voter suppression.

Her body was a text unto itself, displaying the history of brutality that she had suffered, and she used her voice to not let hate get the last word, but to speak of how we might operate, live, and move beyond hate. She often sang before speaking and prayed afterwards, creating her own worship service amid any larger event going on. Harry Belafonte, one of her friends, said,

> I can't describe her voice as a voice. I have got to always talk about Fannie Lou Hamer singing and the power of her voice because there was a mission behind it and in it. I can describe Marilyn Horne, and I can describe Leontyne Price. [The] closest might be Mahalia Jackson, because certainly when Mahalia sang, there was mission in her song, especially when she sang anywhere in the movement.[33]

When people talk about hearing her speak, one thing is consistent—a dynamic articulated by Earnest Bracey: "If nothing else, Hamer suggested something quite significant and practical in terms of solving racial problems. Her magnetic personality and tired, serious eyes drew almost everyone's attention. . . . It was difficult for anyone to forget Hamer after hearing her speak."[34] Her extemporaneous style was not about a linear exposition or a perfectly outlined sermon; rather, she offered anecdotal evidence, supported by biblical framing and invitation, with a clear message for her hearers to be a part of the solution even when it was hard.

This chapter explores her preaching in two different artifacts: "We Haven't Arrived Yet" and "We're on Our Way." These artifacts are intentionally taken from early in her speaking career (1964) and later on (1976) to see the continuities across time. As previously mentioned, I assert that three homiletical insights stem from Hamer: storytelling as a strategy of truth, the constant use of "we" as a proclamation of collective responsibility, and theological and scriptural assertions as a foundation for critique. The artifacts studied here were given at two very different times in her journey, as well as in different settings and to different audiences. As a result, the common trends across the two are indicative of the meta-codes of her rhetoric.

"We're on Our Way" was delivered to a group of Black Mississippians in September 1964 in Indianola, Mississippi, just a few months after Hamer's appearance at the DNC. For upwards of two years she had been trying, with the help of her campaign manager, Charles McLaurin, to get a speaking venue, but it wasn't until after her national stage appearance that she was given an opportunity to influence local politics in this way.[35] Mass meetings were gatherings that were critical to the movement because they were an opportunity for folks to hear from activists on the ground and get instruction for how they could participate.

"We Haven't Arrived Yet" was delivered at the University of Wisconsin–Madison on January 29, 1976, to a group of predominantly white listeners. This was a presentation followed by a question-and-answer period. I will focus on the "presentation" portion and show how this homiletical artifact offers insights in relation to the genre of preaching. This was one of Hamer's last public appearances because she was growing more ill and became unable to travel. Both of these homiletical artifacts demonstrate Hamer's unique preaching style and reflect the rhetorical exigency that emerges from the particularities of her story.

Homiletical Insights

Storytelling as a Strategy for Truth-Telling

Storytelling is critical to Fannie Lou Hamer's homiletic. She is most widely known for the ways that she garnered response through detailed testimony, opening up the ears of her hearers to the painful realities of Black people in Mississippi. In addition to personal testimony, she wove historical examples as precedent for her points; in other situations, she combined personal testimony with those historical examples to weave meaning into the "why" of her demands. Storytelling evoked an emotional response from Hamer's hearers as they were faced with detailed accounts of white supremacy in action and charged to do something to change it. Whether she was speaking to Black audiences or in mixed company, Hamer used this rhetorical strategy to push the urgency of her requests and to speak truths that would otherwise be ignored—or perhaps, for those who had not had these experiences, would be seen as too awful and inhumane to be true. This particular homiletical strategy is important through the lenses of exigency and intersectionality because it is through her specific narrative that the sense of urgency is made plain in the rhetoric. It exposed the truth in a way that was undeniable (even if some chose to ignore it), which forced her hearers to make a choice about what to do with that truth instead of arguing against it.

The Sacred Self: Detailed Personal Testimony

In "We're on Our Way," Hamer starts her preaching with, "First, I would like to tell you about myself."[36] In the moments following this declaration, she unpacks her story. Her goal was for listeners to hear truth in her testimony, to see the problem, and to feel encouraged to participate in the solution. She then says, "My name is Mrs. [claiming respect that was not often given to Black women] Fannie Lou Hamer and I live at 626 East Lafayette Street in Ruleville, Mississippi."[37] After establishing who she is (which they already know) and from where she comes (which is important to her story), she continues with narratives of what has happened. Speaking about registering to vote, she recounts, "When we got here to Indianola, to the courthouse, that was the day I saw more policemens [*sic*] with guns than I'd ever seen in my life at one time. They was standing around and I will never forget that day."[38] She continues the story until she gets to their drive home, and being stopped by a patrolman who was watching the bus:

> When we got back to Indianola, the bus driver was charged with driving a bus the wrong color. This is the gospel truth but this bus had been used for years for cotton chopping, cotton picking and to carry people to Florida, to work to make enough to live on in the wintertime to get back here to the cotton fields the next spring and summer. But that day the bus had the wrong color.[39]

Again, she is setting the scene through her narrative, highlighting particular instances that were violent and oppressive in nature, stringing together more than one story so that her hearers will know these experiences are the rule rather than the exception. After this account, she tells a story about her return home and the consequences of simply voting:

> After we got to Ruleville, about five o'clock, Reverend Jeff Sunny drove me out into the rural area where I had been working as a timekeeper and a sharecropper for eighteen years. When I got there, I was already fired. My children met me and told me, said "Momma," said "this man is hot!" Said, "He said you will have to go back and withdraw [your registration] or you will have to leave."[40]

Hamer then recounts an exchange with Marlow, the plantation owner. She ends this story saying: "And I addressed and told him, as we have always had to say, 'Mister,' I say, 'I didn't register for you, I say, I was trying to register for myself.' He said, 'We're not ready for that in Mississippi.' He wasn't ready, but I been ready a long time. I had to leave that same night."[41] Following this, Hamer recounts several acts of violence that resulted from her attempts to vote, including, "On the tenth of September in 1962, sixteen bullets was fired into the home of Mr. and Mrs. Robert Tucker for me."[42]

This first series of personal testimonies in "We're on Our Way" frames the question she truly wants her hearers to answer. The situations she describes cannot continue for her, which gives her now a clear space to pose a question that she has already answered with her testimony: "Now the question I raise: is this America, the land of the free and the home of the brave? Where people are being murdered, lynched and killed because they want to register to vote?"[43] Hamer's testimony stood as a witness to what was wrong and which couldn't be disputed because it was the truth of experience. It was the foundation for her argument, supporting her demands and texturing the picture of what her proclaiming aimed to change. Testimony invites hearers into the urgency of change and her claim that what has been does not have to be what is or what will be.[44]

Stories from History Woven with Stories of Today

In "We Haven't Arrived Yet," Fannie Lou Hamer again uses personal testimony, along with historical events. At this point in her journey, many to whom she was speaking had already heard her story. So, she uses that story and weaves in other narratives from history to point again towards the issue and the need for continued work. Personal witness is not lost but is framed within broader stories—which is still impactful storytelling. When describing how "sick" America is, Hamer says:

> Where millions of folks have been destroyed, stripped black men of their heritage—and Indians and any other minority group—but stripped us from our heritage, taken our names, integrated our families—from the beginnings. . . . My grandmother was a slave and I just had plenty of white blue-eyed uncles. . . . And today telling me, George Wallace, in Boston, Massachusetts that "let the states handle it, and don't bus the kids." Do you realize how sick we are?[45]

Here she uses her own experience, the story of her grandmother who birthed twenty children, only three of whom were not the result of rape by a white man—which meant many of her uncles and aunts were as light as white people. She cleverly points out that the integration of white people and Black people is not something new (speaking to the interracial identity of her uncles and aunts), but now it is inconvenient for Black people to bring it up because it means rights and not oppression. Still talking about integration but focusing on schools, in "We're on Our Way," she says:

> Now I just want to ask one question: how do you think black people, Indian people, and any other oppressed folk feel celebrating something that, years ago, destroyed over twenty-five million of my people that was being brought here on the slave ships of Africa? Wiped out our heritage; raised families by our grandmothers; and taking our name and today saying that it's wrong to bus a child for equal education! See this kind of crap is nothing but an excuse. See, this is an excuse when they talking about you know, "we don't want the kids bused," and folks buying it![46]

Again, using a story to focus on how sick America was everywhere, not just in the South, she talks about Martin Luther King Jr.'s assassination: "You know we supposed to been an example for the rest of the world, but how you think it feel when a man as nonviolent as Dr. Martin Luther King, that preached nothing but love and says it's wrong to kill, he was assassinated in Memphis, Tennessee? But it was people involved in that from the top to the bottom and they didn't all live in the South."[47] Fannie Lou Hamer uses storytelling as tool to gather evidence for her messages: America is sick, we have work to do, and these things are too urgent not to be addressed and changed.

"We" the People: An Intentional Reminder of Collective Response

The use of "we" when talking about the situation at hand and the action required to move forward is a powerful tool because it makes Hamer and her hearers into a single unit: people who are in this together. For those who felt like brutality was an issue only in the South, the use of "we" reminded them that no area of the United States (or the world) was immune to racism. For those who thought that it was enough to listen to her story and acknowledge it as bad, her continual use of "we" demanded a response from everyone listening: Either you choose to act or you choose to ignore, but both are responses, nonetheless. This was strategic because it made the work collective and also reminded those listening that even after all Hamer has been through (as heard in her testimony), she was still working and including others in that work rather than sending others out to do it. Hamer's use of "we" throughout both artifacts was clearly an intentional choice; she says "we" constantly when she could say "I," as in, This is what I think and I believe and I do, so you should too. Her "we" was a reminder of collective struggle, with the hope for collective overcoming. Here I will highlight a few key moments from each artifact to make this point.

In "We're on Our Way," Hamer was speaking to a group of Black people in Mississippi, affirming that "we" (the Black listeners) were actually moving somewhere but still had many places to go. She is also naming what Black people are up against while reframing the rhetoric of hate that was popular on both opposing sides. She says:

> *We* are not fighting against these people because *we* hate them, but *we* are fighting these people because *we* love them and *we're* the only thing that can save them now. *We* are fighting to save these people from their hate and from all the things that would be so bad against them. *We* want them to see the right way. . . . And I believe tonight, that one day in Mississippi—if I have to die for this—*we* shall overcome.[48]

Here she is showing that *we* are fighting, *we* are moving beyond hate—even if hate is what "they" are using. As a result, it isn't "I" who will overcome, but *we*. When speaking of her belief in legislative power as the reason why it is so critical for folks to register to vote, she asserts, "*We* want people, *we* want people over us that's concerned about the people because *we* are human beings. *We* have prayed and have hoped for God to bring about a change. And now the time has come for people to stand up."[49] In her closing, she does use "you" and "I," but makes clear these are for the purposes of "we"—again, strategically reminding listeners that they are being charged to act and that action together allows for a collective journey and reaping together. Hamer closes,

> *We* want ours and *we* want ours now. . . . But *we* are determined today, *we* are determined that one day we'll have the power of the ballot. And the sooner you go to the courthouse, the sooner *we'll* have it. It's one thing, it's one thing I don't want to say tonight after I finish—and it won't be long—I don't want to hear you say, "honey I behind you." Well, move, I don't want you back there. Because you could be two hundred miles behind. I want you to say, "I'm with you." And *we'll* go up this freedom road together.[50]

That was the goal—that freedom would be a gift to the collective—and Hamer's continual use of "we" reminded them that they would not be alone.

In "We Haven't Arrived Yet," Hamer was speaking to a group of mostly white (although still mixed) and educated people in Wisconsin. Her use of "we" here had a similar strategy in reminding them that this was a collective effort. However, this "we" was used both to show the solidarity of the Mississippians she represented, while also promoting a sense of collective urgency about racism, and declaring that despite how the audience might feel, "We are in this together." She proclaims:

> Blacks in the North is in the worse condition, most of them, than we are in the South because we know where we stand! And a lot of you don't. You know some of you get a few degrees, a pretty good house, and a bill you can't hardly pay—trying to live like somebody else and think you have arrived. But, honey, regardless of how you feel, *we* are in this bag together. And there's nobody at the University of Wisconsin and no other place in this country is free until I am free in the South.[51]

While the struggle was seen clearly and in a particular explicit expression of violence in the South, Hamer wanted to be clear that racism in the North was still alive and well in its own way. She reminds her listeners that we are in this together and if any of us are oppressed, we all are. "We" aren't free until we *all* are.

Scripture as Moral Foundation

Fannie Lou Hamer uses many biblical examples in her speaking. A daughter of a Baptist preacher and a lifelong person of faith, she knew the Bible deeply. Even though she spoke extemporaneously, she quoted passages of Scripture often, using them as clear parallels to the problems at hand. To think more specifically about her uses of Scripture and theological assertions, I break them up into three categories: (1) Scripture to show God is on the side of the fight for freedom, (2) Scripture used to critique the church, and (3) Scripture used to critique white America. All of these point to Scripture as a tool that directly parallels life and as a collective moral compass that exposes the issues at hand.

1. Scripture to Show God is on the Side of the Fight for Freedom

In "We're on Our Way," Hamer says, "When my family and I decided to move back in Sunflower County in December, the car that we had been paying on for the last three years, it was taken. We didn't have many things and part of them had been stolen. But just to show you that God wants people to stand up—so, we began at this address, 626 East Lafayette Street."[52] She articulates early that God wants the work to be done, so even though the car was gone they got a house. She places God on the side of the work she is inviting the people to join. After a string of stories, she then says:

> You see the point is about this, and you can't deny it, not either one of you here in this room—Not Negroes—we have prayed for a change in the state of Mississippi for years. And God made it so plain he sent Moses down in Egypt-land to tell Pharaoh to let my people go. And he made it so plain here in Mississippi [that] the man that heads the project is named Moses, Bob Moses. And he sent Bob Moses down in Mississippi, to tell all these hate groups to let his people go.[53]

Even though this wasn't a church service, the use of this Exodus narrative would have been well known in the context of a group of Black people in a church setting. She uses Scripture to place God on their side as an encouragement and as an assertion that this work is God's work.

In "We Haven't Arrived Yet," Hamer references Mark 3:25 to describe the state of the nation. She says:

> See, some of you all aint going to like it because you know, and I am just telling the truth and so you can, you know, you can respect the truth because if changes is not made in this

> sick country, it's not going to be *me* crumbling, *we* are going to crumble, because a house divided against itself cannot stand. A nation that's divided against itself is on its way out and when you see a place that's so prejudiced that anything is divided, you know anything is divided, not only for kids is for grown-ups.[54]

By directly paralleling this Scripture and the nation, Hamer aligns God with the work at hand and explicitly places the forces that are against liberation and freedom in the role of evil. Hamer later asserts, "And the sixth chapter of Ephesians and the eleventh and the twelfth verse said: 'Put on the whole armor of God that he may be able to stand against the wiles of the devil.' And the twelfth verse say: 'For we wrestle not against flesh and blood, but against power. Against principalities. Against the rulers of darkness of this world. Against spiritual wickedness in high places.'"[55] This work is a part of the armor against evil and is the armor of God—so, again, God is on the side of freedom.

2. Scripture to Critique the Church

This use of Scripture primarily shows up in "We're on Our Way," although you can see it in other artifacts and in her question-and-answer time after "We Haven't Arrived Yet." Hamer was known to be frustrated by clergy because she felt that the church could be doing much more than it was doing. "This is one of the things that I don't like," she says. "Every church door in the state of Mississippi should be open for these meetings; but preachers have preached for years what he didn't believe himself. And if he's willing to trust God, if he's willing to trust God, he won't mind opening the church door."[56] Here, she is critiquing preachers' fears of being targeted if they fight for freedom, while naming that freedom is exactly what they have been preaching. She continues,

> Because the first words of Jesus's public ministry was: "The spirit of the Lord is upon me because he has anointed me to preach the gospel to the poor. He has sent me to proclaim and bring relief to the captive." And you know we are living

> in a captivated society today. The thirty-seventh of Psalms said, "Fret not thouselves because of evildoers, neither be thy envious against the workers of iniquity for they shall be cut down like the green grass and wither away as the green herb. Delight thouselves in the Lord and verily thou shalt be filled." And we are determined to be filled in Mississippi today.[57]

Hamer's frustration was that preachers and sometimes church folks claimed things that she did not see them practicing in ways that she found effective: "We know we have a long fight because the leaders like the preachers and the teachers, they are failing to stand up today."[58] She says with frustration,

> Now you can't tell me you trust God and come out to a church every Sunday with a bunch of stupid hats on[,] seeing what the other one have on and paying the preacher's way to hell and yours too. Preachers is really shocking to find them out. You know they like to rear back in the corners and over the rostrum and said, "what God has done for Meshach, Shadrach, and Abednego" but what he didn't know, God has done the same thing for Fannie Lou Hamer, Annell Ponder and Lawrence Guyot.[59]

Talking about a specific preacher she reiterates, "The preacher said, 'I don't like bringing politics into the church.' And when he says this it make me sick because he's telling a big lie because every dollar bill got a politician on it and the preacher love it. And if this man, and if this man don't choose to be a shepherd, he can be a sheep and follow the shepherd."[60]

Hamer names her frustration and then asserts that she knows firsthand what God has done—and that she wants the church to be a part of the solution.

3. Scripture to Critique White America

Hamer also uses Scripture to critique white America. In "We're on Our Way," she says,

> Some of the white people will tell us, well, I just don't believe in integration. But he been integrating at night a

> long time! If he hadn't been, it would [not] be as many light-skinned Negroes as it is in here. The seventeenth chapter of Acts and the twenty-sixth verse said: He has made of one blood all nations. So, whether you black as a skillet or white as a sheet, we are made from the same blood and we are on our way.[61]

Later, the Bible is used to support her claim about the need for Black people to vote and that America must change. Hamer argues,

> America is divided against itself and without their considering us human beings, one day America will crumble. Because God is not pleased. God is not pleased at all the murdering, and all of the brutality, and all the killings for no reason at all. God is not pleased at the Negro children in the State of Mississippi suffering from malnutrition. God is not pleased because we have to go raggedy each day. God is not pleased because we have to go to the field and work from ten to eleven hours for three lousy dollars.[62]

In short: God is not pleased at the state of affairs for Black people as a result of American racism.

Finally, Hamer uplifts Black people using the text, again reminding them of the ways that whiteness is violent to their existence:

> "Righteousness exalts a nation, but sin is a reproach to any people." The beatitude of the Bible, the fifth chapter of Matthew said: "Blessed are they that moan, for they shall be comforted." We have moaned a long time in Mississippi. And he said, the meek shall inherit the earth. And there's no race in America that's no meeker than the Negro. We're the only race in America that has had babies sold from our breast, which was slavery time. And had mothers sold from their babes. And we're the only race in America that had one man had to march through a mob crew just to go to school, which was James H. Meredith. We don't have anything to be ashamed of. All we have to do is trust God and launch into the deep. You can pray until you faint, but if you don't get up and try to do something, God is not going to put it in your lap.[63]

Hamer claims that God is on their side, but also that there is work to be done. She uses Scripture to back her claim that the lives of Black people will get better, but that this will require work from them as well—even as she names ways that white America has made Black lives particularly horrendous.

Conclusion

Fannie Lou Hamer believed that freedom was possible, that justice was not outside of the people's grip, and that her experiences that told her otherwise didn't have to be the story forever—and certainly not for those coming behind her. She spent the latter part of her life publicly advocating for voter registration and ways of mitigating the poverty that was ever present for Black people in Mississippi. Her willingness to tell her story in uncut ways, to demand that "we" be foundational to the work, and to speak to the masses using Scripture as a parallel to the world and therefore a tool for critique, comprise the particular homiletic insights offered by her unique perspective—insights that we can all listen to and learn from. Her rhetoric, rooted in the experiences of what had been, the work in which she was engaged, and a vision of a future that she believed in moving towards, shows the nature of preaching from her perspective. Her unwillingness to compromise in ways that lessened the blow of her truth was the gift of her rhetoric and her preaching fervor.

Fannie Lou Hamer's rhetoric was a product of her story and emerged from her practices of bringing forth the freedoms she talked about so passionately. Her preaching responded to the life that she was living and her hope for a better tomorrow. Her preaching was uniquely hers. Hamer's homiletical strategies offer new tools to consider when thinking about preaching outside of the institutional church and in different settings. When speaking about her preaching, hearers could not deny that her witness made them think and at least consider what she was saying because it was based in so much unadulterated truth.[64] She called for America to see the truth of its sickness and, in the same breath, to know that where we are doesn't have to be where we remain. She believed deeply in freedom, recognizing it would take everyone's action to get there and that America had to change. As Hamer asserted:

> There's so much hypocrisy in America. The land of the free and the home of the brave is all on paper. It doesn't mean anything to us. The only way we can make this thing a reality in America is to do all we can to destroy this system and bring this thing out to the light that has been under the cover all these years. The scriptures have said, "The things done in the dark will be known on the house tops."[65]

5
Conclusion

A Homiletical Hermeneutic of Particularity: Insights of Black Women's Non-Pulpit Preaching

Sojourner Truth, Nannie Helen Burroughs, and Fannie Lou Hamer teach us so much about the possibilities and practices of preaching through their proclamation. Black women preachers proclaiming on platforms outside of the pulpit bring a critically new perspective and voice to homiletics. Their preaching was not and is not limited to Sunday morning service, but expands across each day of the week, advocating for the freedom and flourishing of Black people. Through their witness, we see that preaching is not about the location of the pulpit or the institutional backing that is often required for individuals to take a space in that pulpit. Black women's non-pulpit preaching is a practice of proclaiming the hope for justice as truth, oriented towards moving the society to a more beloved place of wholeness and possibility, rooted in freedom and the care of those on whom their witness is focused. Such preaching proposes immediate change. These preaching women didn't have the luxury of vague or abstract messaging, after which hearers would leave without knowing what they were being asked to do. They spoke with clarity and conviction, aimed towards specific goals—conviction that today invites us to consider the nature and purpose of preaching in a new light. Sojourner Truth, Nannie Helen Burroughs, and Fannie Lou Hamer practiced preaching with the telos of justice from their viewpoint in the here and now, in direct response to the specific needs they were experiencing. Their preaching practice was rooted in a change they envisioned that day, because urgency was at the forefront for their communities. Their words and witness demonstrate unique homiletical insights, rooted in their lives and immediate situations, which required urgent action.

Their contribution to the discipline of homiletics starts with centering the voices that have been excluded from the study of preaching. For several reasons, these preachers have often been left out of our courses of study. First, even those Black women preachers who managed to gain access to pulpits haven't been widely studied. Patriarchy continues to serve as a gatekeeper to Black women's access to pulpit spaces, and although the study of the preaching of Black women has expanded among different Black women homileticians, it is still far from equitable in relation to their male counterparts. In addition, even though Black women are being studied, the location of preaching has still been primarily in the institutional church and in formal worship services. When the study of preaching is solely or even primarily engaged as a pulpit practice, we risk the erasure of the fullness of Black women's preaching practice, along with so many others whose voices have been marginalized or who have been excluded from the pulpit. This intervention challenges the notion that preaching is limited to any space, particularly one with a history of exclusion.[1] Finally, when we only study contemporary voices, we miss out on the gift of lineage for those who find themselves on expansive platforms. It matters to have those who have come before us, whom we can listen to and learn from. We have much to learn from the homiletical witness of Sojourner Truth, Nannie Helen Burroughs, and Fannie Lou Hamer, who are Black women non-pulpit preachers.

A Homiletical Hermeneutic of Particularity, Intersectionality, and Exigency

This book uses biography as a fulcrum for understanding the homiletical rhetoric of Truth, Burroughs, and Hamer in order to illuminate the ways that their embodiment and lived experience were critical to their rhetoric. Black women non-pulpit preachers all speak from a homiletical hermeneutic of *particularity, intersectionality, and exigency.* A homiletical hermeneutic of particularity, intersectionality, and exigency (PIE) is a lens through which a preacher's markers of identity converge with specific responses to her context and the world around her and become the interpretive tool for her preaching. These women—whom we tend not to hear because they've been marginalized in society and from the pulpit—and their specific lived particularities teach us about why particularities matter in general, why their specific circumstances bear exigency for the world and the gospel, and why it is problematic to exclude the voices that bring these particularities to the forefront of preaching. These women become a paradigm for why our understanding of preaching should be expanded beyond the pulpit, why particularities matter for the preaching of truth, and why marginalized voices should not be excluded. These preachers see the world through their experiences and narratives, and through their hopes for a better world for their specific communities. Sojourner Truth spoke as a previously enslaved Black woman from New York, a heritage through which she interpreted women's suffrage and the rights of Black people. She often spoke to mixed or primarily white audiences, which shaped how she spoke and what she said. Nannie Helen Burroughs began speaking at twenty-one years old and had a long career across decades. Her primary speaking was in Baptist circles and educational spaces. Although sometimes she spoke in mixed spaces, she primarily addressed Black people in her quest for Black women's forward movement, especially in regard to Black women domestic workers and those seen as "less than" even within the Black community. Fannie Lou Hamer came from Mississippi and talked about the ways that her socioeconomic status set her apart from other aspects of the movement in which she participated. She spoke through the story of her lived experiences of violence and other injustices she was fighting. All three of these Black non-pulpit preachers demonstrate that their proclamation was rooted in their lives.

In the previous chapters, I explored the unique homiletical practices that defined the preaching of each of these women individually. However, while they have unique homiletical practices, there are key overarching homiletical insights to consider as well. Each insight is posed as a question because studying these preachers gives us possibility—not only in our notions of what preaching is, but also in the invitation to all Black women preachers to consider their own preaching voices, the nature and purpose of who they are as preachers, and the context in which they choose to proclaim. All of these insights demonstrate that each preacher has a voice stemming from particularity.

Black women's non-pulpit preaching opens up several possibilities. Their preaching is rooted first in context, with a goal of responding to the exigency at hand so that some change might result from the rhetoric brought forth. For each of these preachers, the starting point of preaching was herself and the world she inhabited, and everything else was interpreted through the lens of that experiencing—offering others a piece of that truth through an invitation to practice. Through engaging their Blackness, their womanness, and the other markers of their lives, they created and engaged particular rhetorical situations. By listening to the witness of Black women non-pulpit preachers, preachers in general must consider their own particularity as critical to their preaching, not divorced from it. In addition, the spectrum of places for preaching, and who is included both in our contemporary understandings and our historical lineages of preaching, will continue to expand. Out of the homiletical hermeneutic of particularity we gain insights into the sanctity of story, the exigent function, the critical importance of practices that parallel preaching, and Scripture and theology as a moral compass.

The Sanctity of Your Story: How Does Your Story Serve the Purpose of Your Preaching?

Black women non-pulpit preachers teach us the significance of personal narrative in proclamation. Their embodiment as Black women and their experience of the times and places in which they were living were not addendums or cute illustrations but the heart and substance of their preaching. These women used their life stories as both an effective tool for displaying the current circumstance and as a means of explaining a response to make that situation better. As people who were marginalized, their stories were often ignored or not told, and therefore bearing witness to their own lives and the lives of those around them who were also oppressed was central to their invitation to their hearers.

In different ways, Sojourner Truth, Nannie Helen Burroughs, and Fannie Lou Hamer utilized their own stories and embodiment to provide concreteness to the messages they were speaking. Sojourner Truth points us to her womanhood as a Black woman and calls out injustice particular to her embodiment. She used her experience as a previously enslaved woman to expound her claims that women have rights—and that means *all* women. Nannie Helen Burroughs pulled from the narratives of what she witnessed firsthand as a domestic worker. By hearing her story, we become aware of how that story was woven into her sense of urgency to develop a higher level of societal respect and access for all Black women, especially those who (like domestic workers) have been overlooked. Fannie Lou Hamer's rhetorical prowess centered her story as the sacred text of truth, refusing to shy away from details of her pain that might have made others uncomfortable, as a practice of bearing witness to the things she was fighting against. All three highlight their stories in their own way, yet the common thread is that their story is sacred and has authority, that their truth is worth proclaiming, and that this is foundational to their preaching.

Centering their story as sacred also expands and reinforces the collective memory of the hearers. Even if hearers previously hadn't known the reality of the conditions being described by these preachers, the hearers are now responsible for having that information. A story that is not yours may be easier to ignore or deny as truth, but none of these preachers' hearers can deny that they have been told there is something that can be done to change the realities. In *Preaching as Testimony*, Anna Carter Florence argues:

> Preaching in the tradition of testimony shifts the locus of authority away from the ministerial office and places it with

> the one who testifies: that is, the one who has seen and believed the liberating power of God's Word and who then risks proclaiming the truth of the gospel. This shift locates authentic and authoritative preaching not in the ecclesial center but in particular situations of struggle and trial at the margins, in which competing worldviews and even lives might be at stake.[2]

Black women non-pulpit preachers find themselves in this testimonial tradition, already pushing against normative ideas of who can preach and what the ministerial office contains. However, while these preachers use God's word written in text, they lean on God's lived word through the sacred "text" of their experiences. The *struggle* Florence talks about occupies the center of their narratives. Authority migrates from the singular witness of the biblical text towards the witness of the sacred text of their lived struggles for justice. It is this authority that grounds their agency to continue writing and speaking. Their struggles are central to their accounts of their lived experiences and the lived experiences of those with and for whom they advocate, resisting the racist, sexist, and often classist worldviews of the environments in which they live. In their use of story as a tool of proclamation, they claim space and highlight a new tradition where who they are and what they have experienced is central to their sacred proclamation. They use story as both declaration and invitation for their audience to respond, which stirs a liberating force that resists and challenges the normative power structures that have made the realities they aim to change possible in the first place. The stories and testimonies are the sacred text of their narratives, supported by other "texts" woven in to complete the message. These Black women non-pulpit preachers teach all Black women preachers to excavate and consider our stories worth telling as a part of sacred truth and for the purposes of the preaching impact. This impact aims at increasing freedom, justice, and collective belovedness, especially for those who have not been given the luxury of these things from the systems they inhabit.

As a result of listening to Truth, Burroughs, and Hamer, all marginalized preachers might consider the question, How does my story serve the purpose of my preaching? Preachers are often made to feel tied to interpreting the biblical text, the contemporary context (today's news and the social location of the local community), and cultural references that would translate to the community of listeners. However, the specificity of personal witness and testimony as critical to one's homiletical structure is an offering from these non-pulpit preachers. Typically, "witness" and "testimony" in a preaching context is considered through expressions of "what Jesus has done for me," but these women are speaking witness to what has happened in their lives as something important to hear on its own terms. Jesus is not stripped from the narrative entirely, but their own encounter with God is no less important. This kind of truth telling is still rooted in the power of God for them, but that power is referential to their lived experiences and the ways they believe that change can occur as a result of preaching. They expand the notion of testimony in that it can also serve as an invitation to participate in God's activity of justice in this world.

This question also invites preachers to consider which stories are almost always or almost never told. As Black women preachers, Truth's, Burroughs's, and Hamer's stories were often cast aside and not considered. By centering their stories, these preachers made known what had been pushed to the margins. Speaking their stories reveals what has not been heard, even as the speaking itself pushes against the norms of what "should" be heard. Black women preachers must consider how their stories are shaped within the larger context to determine their effective use, especially how the use of their story might be subversive and oriented to the work of justice. Not all stories function the same way. That is why the question asks how one's story can be used towards the goal of preaching, which is wholeness, justice, and freedom. The question from this insight doesn't aim to move preachers to ask, How can we include more personal narratives in the sermon? but, How can I use my personal narrative to increase belovedness, wholeness, possibility, freedom, justice? For some non-Black, non-marginalized people, the answer may be that their personal narrative needs to be one of repentance and reparation, for example, and not one in which their own personal story is centered in the same way as these women in their preaching. Not all white, male, privileged, ordained preachers—or preachers who possess any other identity markers that are rooted in access and privilege—should or even could tell their personal stories as a means to proclaim a truth that moves the community towards freedom and justice. When one's story is already centered within the dominant culture, a different way of using narrative may be the most effective means towards reaching the aforementioned goals. Not all personal narratives demonstrate exigency or illuminate justice, so it is critical that preachers find the ways in which their personal narrative aligns with these purposes of preaching.

By narrating their contextualized struggles for justice, non-pulpit preachers centralize and mobilize their own stories as equally sacred alongside the other stories being woven together for the purposes of the message. However, context matters, and preachers should consider how to approach this in their own settings. Again, these are Black women non-pulpit preachers whose stories were not readily told. When Sojourner Truth articulates the specifics of her hard labor and work in the field, which for white women would have been considered men's work, she does so to parallel her humanity with those trying to deny it, prompting them to consider her question, "Am I not also a human being and a woman as well?" When Nannie Helen Burroughs names the lived experiences of domestic working women, she does so as one who has done that work and seen her mother and grandmother do so as well. The goal is to garner honor so that more resources can be provided for this group that has been cast aside. When Fannie Lou Hamer tells the detailed narratives of her beating at the Winona prison, she paints a concrete picture for her hearers of the horrors that they have agency to respond to and change. Her story aimed to open minds and hearts for the purposes of action. These stories are sacred, as they enliven and point towards the message of justice and the invitation to participate in its coming as a part of God's activity in the world.

Exigent Function: To What Are You Responding, and How Are You Asking Your Hearers to Respond?

These Black women non-pulpit preachers carved out expansive platforms for their proclamation. Whether they were speaking to thousands or just a handful of people, the sense of urgency was the same. They weren't speaking in abstract ideas or inaccessible metaphors to a "universal" audience. Their preaching responded directly to a specific problem that they aimed to change. The telos of their preaching was clear: an actionable response. Their rhetoric did not leave the end goal up to the imagination of the hearer because it was far too important. Lives were literally at stake. Their preaching practice was a response to an immediate situation that needed to be addressed; the function of the preaching was in the here and now, rooted in justice and an inbreaking of God in their moment, not in the eschatological beyond. Context is paramount in the content, because urgent need is not without particularity but rooted in it.

Exigency worked in two ways for Sojourner Truth, Nannie Helen Burroughs, and Fannie Lou Hamer, which helps us think expansively about preaching. On one end, they were responding to an urgent need of their community that they wanted addressed. As such, they used rhetoric to invite hearers to accept the exigency they were proclaiming as a catalyst for action. Each preacher made clear that she was looking for tangible change, not simply a "knowing." Sojourner Truth was responding as a Black woman in a world where neither Black rights nor women's rights were equal to white men's rights. She wanted women's rights *and* Black rights in a time when neither were supported. To ensure that Black women would not be lost in the pushes for those rights, her aim was to reveal the issues and the absurdity of it all while standing in her fullness as a Black woman; she declared, "Give women their rights." Nannie Helen Burroughs was responding to the harsh conditions of domestic labor occupations that were primary spaces of employment for Black women, as well as the ways these women were looked down upon and seen as "less than" within the Black community itself. In addition, she was responding to racism and sexism (among other things) that created a host of injustices, which then became the catalysts for her creation of clubs and other organizations. Her rhetoric about these conditions was a response to them and a means to get others to respond with their actions. Her preaching always had practical invitations and a reminder that if you weren't going to actively help, at least don't get in the way of progress. Fannie Lou Hamer was responding to the conditions of Black people in Mississippi, noting that oftentimes the voices of poor Black people, especially those who were uneducated and in the South, were being left out of the conversation. She used her rhetoric as a response to these conditions and then named responses for her hearers: There is no *not* responding to the situation of Black poor people in the Mississippi Delta, and everyone has a role they can play in bringing forth more justice. These women preached towards new action, believing in a world that could be built by those who were listening.

With exigency in the forefront, Black women preachers might ask themselves, What am I responding to now? and, How am I asking my listeners to respond in concrete ways? The world around these Black women presented urgent situations. They chose to respond, lifting up their voices as Black women from the margins and creating a space where none had been made for them. Preachers might consider what action they want their preaching to inspire and how they hope that action affects their community in a way that creates more justice, belovedness, and freedom for all—especially those for whom society doesn't make room. It's critical that all preachers know that we are all responding to urgent conditions, whether directly from our narrative or in the community around us that is too often a casualty of various forms of privilege. The idea of "calling" and "being called to preach," then, becomes an invitation to participate in the inbreaking of God for a clear purpose: response that positively impacts the whole, not just those for whom things are easy or comfortable. "Call" is not an abstract invitation from God, but a call from God to an actual situation in order to bring more justice, hope, and freedom to this earth, enlivening the possibilities of more freedom for all.

The telos of non-pulpit preaching is always pragmatic and tied to a concreteness of real issues, which creates room for a proclaiming space to emerge. Marginalized preachers across platforms should consider these questions, so that listeners are invited to participate in a new world through their actions. In addition, such preachers must wrestle with how they are articulating the urgency for action, as these women have shown us that the right time to respond in the face of injustice is always now. Black women non-pulpit preachers show us the benefit of exigent response to preaching. It enlivens action and pushes rhetoric from the abstract to the actualized, animated in the practices of hearers.

The Practices That Parallel Preaching: How Do Your Practices Align with Your Proclamation?

Black women's non-pulpit preaching emerges from their practice, aiming to inspire the practice and work of others for the sake of a more just world as seen above in the exigent function. The study of preaching has primarily been rooted in the moment of oratorical offering to a group of listeners. The hope is certainly that preachers are living what they are proclaiming, but the tangible evidence of that is not always clear. Through the preaching witness of Truth, Burroughs, and Hamer we see what preaching looks like when practice forms and supports preaching. Knowing the story of these preachers, alongside listening to their rhetoric, we see clearly that their rhetoric was backed up by habits of action—strong and often collectively shared practices. They were already engaged in and practicing what they were asking others to do. This is critical because this invitation holds proclaimers accountable to their words beyond the rhetorical situation. It requires an authenticity that can be seen by those listening, which then compels the listeners to respond with action of their own—ideally practices that increase justice and freedom.

Truth, Burroughs, and Hamer engaged in specific, goal-oriented actions that were in direct alignment with their preaching. Sojourner Truth demanded respect and an acknowledgment of her humanity, which she first gave herself. In renaming herself beyond her previously enslaved self, she used her agency and made clear that she would acknowledge her own journey; her renaming was a declaration of her fight for more freedom through the journey to truth. Nannie Helen Burroughs advocated for the education of Black women, access to more resources for Black people at large, and a church that would see itself as a resource for Black flourishing every day, not only Sunday. As such, she built a school supported by Black funding to show that Black women can build things and can support themselves to gain access to what they need. She also created organizations for Black women to find community and to be able to serve in ministry where they had otherwise been unable to do so. Again, she didn't simply talk about these things, telling others what they should and should not do; her practices shaped her rhetoric such that she was able to speak truth from what she knew and invite others to join her and do their part, unique to their own particularity. Fannie Lou Hamer continuously put her body and life on the line for what she believed in: Black voting rights and economic support for Black people. Her request for others to sacrifice wasn't without a bodily memory of what her request could mean, and her plea that those listening advocate for poor Black people in Mississippi—not just certain Black people—came from her experience of doing that work as a poor Black person in Mississippi and using what little resources she had to make change. For all three, the praxis of preaching emerged from what they were doing, emphasizing that their rhetoric was rooted in that truth.

Preachers might ask themselves, Am I preaching for an actual response? Again, if not, that is something to be addressed because preaching aims towards response. As Lisa Thompson asserts in *Ingenuity*, "Namely we are left with the criteria that preaching does not exist for the sake of itself, but somehow preaching is accountable to life on the ground because life itself is sacred."[3] For Black women non-pulpit preachers, this accountability is more than just an ear to the ground by reading the newspaper. This is an ethical commitment to preaching from your lived and practiced truth, and to not preaching *at* people with requirements that you as preacher have no intention of living into. For the three Black women preachers I studied, this looked like activism and pushing for new policies, resources, and opportunity for the Black community. However, this commitment is not limited to these particular types of practice. Sermons focused on self-care should come from someone practicing wellness, not just talking about it. Preaching that invites stewardship should come from practices of alignment and stewardship beyond money: with time, people, and other resources that allow for life. Preaching and practice should not be disparate in the life of the proclaimer. Preaching is not only an act of teaching or proclamation or even testimony but of living the things that preaching proclaims about how the world is supposed to be. Black women non-pulpit preachers show us an embodied version of preaching that aligns the personhood of the preacher with the act of preaching and claims that that personhood is central to the truth of the proclamation that aims towards justice and freedom.

Scripture and Theology as Moral Compass: How Do Scripture and Our View of God Support the Work of Justice?

Black women non-pulpit preachers use Scripture as familiar points of reference to create new parallels with concrete, contemporary situations. For non-pulpit preachers, the exegetical exposition that we might expect in pulpit preaching is not required. But for these preachers, Scripture was in many ways a moral compass, reaffirming their assertions about action with theological and scriptural backing. God was on the side of those who would take action that aligned with the work the preachers were proposing. Throughout the preaching of these women, their theological claims consistently aligned their work with a call from God, and the reasoning behind their invitations to their hearers was rooted in Scripture. One of the things we learn is that the ways they rhetorically engaged their particularity required both *a lens and response* of justice. We can learn from these preachers how we can read and attend to our own particularities through a lens of justice and then align our scriptural and theological uses towards justice, as well.

Both Fannie Lou Hamer and Sojourner Truth were extemporaneous preachers, pulling scriptural references from memory to use as theological backing for practical assertions throughout their preaching. Although Nannie Helen Burroughs was less extemporaneous, her use of Scripture was similar in that pieces were taken from throughout the Bible to support her point and create pragmatic parallels to what she was claiming about the world. Truth specifically engaged Scripture to cultivate expansive memory, bringing in new ideas woven with her experience, such that the text was heard in a new way by her (often white) hearers. Burroughs used Scripture as a historical precedent, placing women like Miriam among biblical "greats" to remind her hearers that what she was advocating—the inclusion of women—was not new and was always critical. Fannie Lou Hamer used Scripture as the foundation of her visualization of how the world should operate. Scripture was the underpinning of her critiques of the world around her: How can we live like *this*, when the text says *this*? Hamer referenced many different texts within any given sermon, stringing them together in the service of her overall message: God wants Black people to be free and is behind this work we are doing—so let's do it. Each of them used the text and her placement of God's activity as a moral compass, asserting what was right and what was wrong through the examples from the biblical text.

In reflecting on these Black women non-pulpit preachers, preachers might ask, How is Scripture guiding my preaching towards justice? Where have I positioned God? All of the women in this book imagined God on the side of their work towards more freedom and more equitable living opportunities for Black people in general and for the specific communities they were fighting for within the larger Black community. This was clear in their rhetoric.

Preachers must consider where they see God's activity in the fight for justice and freedom and whether they are committed to articulating that activity clearly in their preaching practice. Black women non-pulpit preachers demonstrate God's divine support as they ask folks to respond practically. God is concerned with the everyday and lived struggles that are exacerbated by systemic oppression, and God is on the side of those fighting for justice. That affirmation is clear to these preachers—an important assertion for anyone preaching to consider.

These questions also allow for preachers to concretize the telos of preaching and to consider their own theological commitments and how those emerge in their preaching. This will shape their exegetical work if that's a part of their preaching practice. For non-pulpit preachers, these questions are critical because an exposition of any one story may not be effective for their goals of action. A threading of multiple stories may provide a stronger basis for a clear moral backing, via the biblical text, for the assertions being made. Scripture, sacred text, and God being on the side of the work for freedom are critical in the language and goals of Black women's non-pulpit preaching. If preachers across platforms engage these questions, they might find clearer theological messages and also offer their listeners clarity on how they are participating in God's work through the invitation of the sermon.

Conclusion

Black women non-pulpit preachers offer the gift of particularity amid exigency, creating a specific lens for their proclamation that has direct and practical implications for the societies in which they live and the communities to which they are accountable. Specifically, from Sojourner Truth, Nannie Helen Burroughs, and Fannie Lou Hamer we recover and uncover new truths when the lived narrative is woven with the scriptural one, such that a new gospel, a new mission, and a new commission are birthed. Preaching is a practice of proclaiming truth, oriented towards moving the community of listeners beyond their current practices and ways of being and into a place of more freedom and possibilities of justice for those who have not had them. When we listen to the preaching and note the rhetorical insights from Black women's non-pulpit preaching, our preaching actually changes. New questions arise, and new ways of thinking about what we are doing and why we are doing it emerge in ways that enhance and further the study of preaching.

I came into this book with a question that will forever change the way I teach and practice preaching, and my aim is that it also changes how the field of homiletics thinks about preaching. How would the study of preaching change if rhetorical studies were centered on Black women's proclamation, including those who weren't often called preachers because they were not located in the pulpit?

This is the beginning of a conversation, not the end of one. This work isn't limited to Sojourner Truth, Nannie Helen Burroughs, and Fannie Lou Hamer. Studying preaching through the lens of Black women non-pulpit preachers opens up a new threshold to possible inquiries into the nature and purpose of preaching as seen across a myriad of platforms, exploring these insights of preaching by studying other non-pulpit Black women preachers in different realms: singers, poets, educators, activists, and nonprofit organizers—in short, whoever found themselves outside of the pulpit but still preaching. This type of inquiry opens up an array of possibilities to consider what preaching is, what its purpose is, and how this expansive view can be taught. It also sparks the question of the liturgical practices that surround these non-pulpit preaching moments and how they might add to the study of ritual and liturgical studies. The expansion of preaching beyond the pulpit is necessary to envision ways of thinking about preaching on platforms not directly connected to worship services, and in many cases without an institutional church affiliation.

In our contemporary world, preachers span many places and spaces. In addition, while the localized church is still critically important, individuals are finding sacred space in other places and ritual environments in which preaching is critical in different and nuanced ways. Preaching is a practice that includes the pulpit but has never been, and never will be, limited to a single platform or a single demographic in order to be alive and dynamic. Listening to the practice and proclaiming of Sojourner Truth, Nannie Helen Burroughs, and Fannie Lou Hamer expands our knowledge of what preaching can be and what we might pay attention to when listening to preachers. Their insights also reveal new questions we in homiletics might consider when thinking about what preaching is, what it means to be "called" to preach, and the critical nature of context in sermon formation.

The gift of a homiletical hermeneutic of particularity, intersectionality, and exigency that rests on the aforementioned four pillars is that preaching is a practice woven with one's person and story, not devoid of it. Too often in pulpit preaching, Black women preachers are taught to focus primarily on the gospel of Jesus, as if who they are is not critical to their proclaiming. It is actually critical for preachers whose voices have been on the margins to take inventory of who they are and preach from a place of particularity so that their stories are woven into the sacred memory of those whose stories are most spoken. Preaching isn't stripped of the self; it quite literally emerges from the self, woven through the expansive nature of a call that uses words spoken aloud. One's unique circumstances and ways of being carve out a particularly rhetorical rhythm that has attachments and threads connected to others, but that stands on its own.

Black women's preaching, especially beyond the pulpit, shows us the necessity of the real presence of the self in the preaching moment and the ways that self-disclosure, personal experience, and the clear assertion of who one is are a strong foundation for the rhetoric one uses and therefore the invitation one offers the hearers. Black women's non-pulpit preaching invites us to consider more ways to listen and understand preaching. In an anti-Black, anti-woman, anti-poor world, Sojourner Truth, Nannie Helen Burroughs, and Fannie Lou Hamer chose to find the audacity to speak prolifically for causes they believed in and placed what they were saying alongside what they were doing. These preachers, moving through different platforms but with clear messages rooted in justice and the hope for Black flourishing, teach us so much about preaching. Their words, proclaimed across a myriad of platforms, are reminders of the expansive nature of preaching and the gospel of truth declaring justice and freedom as its goal. Their invitation reminds me to be bold and expansive in my own proclaiming practice and do all I can to invite others to do the same. This is their homiletic. And as the church folks would say, "That'll preach."

NOTES

1 Introduction

1 Lloyd F. Bitzer, "The Rhetorical Situation," *Philosophy & Rhetoric* 1, no. 1 (1968): 6, https://www.jstor.org/stable/40236733.

2 Bitzer, "The Rhetorical Situation," 6.

3 Bitzer, "The Rhetorical Situation," 8.

4 Bitzer, "The Rhetorical Situation," 13.

5 For more on the term and its published beginnings, see Kimberle Crenshaw, "Mapping the Margins: Intersectionality, Identity Politics, and Violence Against Women of Color," *Stanford Law Review* 43, no. 6 (1991): 1241–99, https://www.jstor.org/stable/1229039.

6 Patricia Hill Collins and Sirma Bilge, *Intersectionality* (Cambridge: Polity, 2016), 2.

7 Collins and Bilge, *Intersectionality*, 42.

8 Emilie Townes writes: "The key for womanist theology is the use of an interstructured analysis employing class, gender, and race. This kind of analysis is both descriptive (an analysis and sociohistorical perspective of Black life and Black religious worldviews) and prescriptive (offering suggestions for the eradication of oppression in the lives of African Americans, and by extension, the rest of humanity and creation)." Emilie M. Townes, "Womanist Theology," *Union Seminary Quarterly Review* 57, no. 3 (2003): 159. This womanist, interstructured analysis to which Townes refers is present in the tool of intersectionality, especially with a careful look at race, gender, and class. In other methodologies, these different identities (race, gender, class) might be studied separately, while potentially noting overlap. However, when one's embodiment includes all of them, the luxury to extricate any from the others isn't present.

9 While some might suggest other scholars who could be added to this group, the works selected offer a sufficient sample size to support the assertion being made about the overall scholarship on Black preaching.

10 Henry H. Mitchell, *Black Preaching: The Recovery of a Powerful Art* (Nashville: Abingdon, 1990), 34.

11 Cleophus J. LaRue, *The Heart of Black Preaching* (Louisville: Westminster John Knox, 2000), 6.

12 LaRue, *Heart of Black Preaching*, 20.

13 Luke A. Powery, *Spirit Speech* (Nashville: Abingdon, 2009), 96.

14 There are nuances in the language of "Black" versus "African American" preaching, but for this book I will use "Black preaching" and "African American preaching" interchangeably. When I quote the work of other authors who use "African American preaching," I honor their choice of language.

15 Kenyatta R. Gilbert, *The Journey and Promise of African American Preaching* (Minneapolis: Fortress, 2011), 12.

16 Gilbert, *Journey and Promise*, 14.

17 Christine M. Smith, *Weaving the Sermon: Preaching in a Feminist Perspective* (Louisville: Westminster John Knox, 1989), 110.

18 Rose's model responds to John S. McClure's *The Roundtable Pulpit: Where Leadership and Preaching Meet* (Nashville: Abingdon, 1995).

19 Lucy Atkinson Rose, *Sharing the Word: Preaching in the Roundtable Church* (Louisville: Westminster John Knox, 1997), 4.

20 Mary Donovan Turner and Mary Lin Hudson, *Saved from Silence: Finding Women's Voice in Preaching* (St. Louis: Lucas Park Books, 2014), 61.

21 Anna Carter Florence, *Preaching as Testimony* (Louisville: Westminster John Knox, 2007), 4.

22 Florence, *Preaching as Testimony*, xxvi–xxvii.

23 Beverly Zink-Sawyer, *From Preachers to Suffragists: Woman's Rights and Religious Conviction in the Lives of Three Nineteenth-Century American Clergywomen* (Louisville: Westminster John Knox, 2003).

24 Roxanne Mountford, *The Gendered Pulpit: Preaching in American Protestant Spaces* (Carbondale: Southern Illinois University Press, 2005).

25 Teresa L. Fry Brown, *Weary Throats and New Songs: Black Women Proclaiming God's Word* (Nashville: Abingdon, 2003), 21.

26 In *Katie's Canon*, womanist ethicist Katie Cannon asserts, "A womanist critique of homiletics challenges conventional biblical interpretations of sin-bringing Eve, wilderness-whimpering Hagar, henpecking Jezebel, whoring Gomer, prostituting Mary Magdalene and conspiring Sapphira." See Katie Cannon, *Katie's Canon: Womanism and the Soul of the Black Community* (New York: Continuum, 1995), 114.

27 For a full list of what constitutes a womanist homiletic, see Donna E. Allen, *Toward a Womanist Homiletic: Katie Cannon, Alice Walker and Emancipatory Proclamation* (New York: Lang, 2013), 43–44.

28 Allen, *Toward a Womanist Homiletic*, 27.

29 Lisa L. Thompson, *Ingenuity: Preaching as an Outsider* (Nashville: Abingdon, 2018), 175.

30 Thompson, *Ingenuity*, 45.

31 It is important to note that preaching as defined in the New Testament was not oriented around a particular place. Preaching words such as *kerygma*, often translated to "preaching," were about the task itself. "Pulpit" was a much later concept, yet the notions of proclamation and witness to the ongoing work of God and the invitation to participate were still present. There are several words that have been translated in the New Testament text as "preaching," but none of them demand that there is a particular place for proclamation to occur. Contemporary notions of preaching have continually narrowed into the specificities of the pulpit.

32 Jeanne Halgren Kilde, *Sacred Power, Sacred Space: An Introduction to Christian Architecture and Worship* (New York: Oxford University Press, 2008), 7.

33 Kilde, *Sacred Power, Sacred Space*, 24.

34 Mountford, *Gendered Pulpit*, 8.

35 Mountford, *Gendered Pulpit*, 6.

36 Mountford, *Gendered Pulpit*, 98.

37 John S. McClure, *The Four Codes of Preaching: Rhetorical Strategies* (Louisville: Westminster John Knox, 2003), 9.

38 McClure, *Four Codes of Preaching*, 15–16.

39 I would edit this code slightly and call it the "sacred text" code and/or still call it the scriptural code but be explicit in naming its expansive nature. As Christian traditions expand and as different marginal voices find sacred identity in extracanonical texts, their use and exegetical work with those texts still aid in the support and unpacking of this coding system.

40 McClure, *Four Codes of Preaching*, 57.

41 McClure, *Four Codes of Preaching*, 96–97.

42 McClure, *Four Codes of Preaching*, 93.

43 McClure, *Four Codes of Preaching*, 136.

44 We see this is explicitly in John S. McClure's later works, *Speaking Together and with God: Liturgy and Communicative Ethics* (Lanham, MD: Lexington Books, 2018) and *Mashup Religion: Pop Music and Theological Invention* (Waco, TX: Baylor University Press, 2011).

45 It does not escape me that I am a Black woman scholar engaging the voice and coding system of a white male scholar to consider the preaching voices of the Black women to whom I am listening. To be clear, *The Four Codes* provides a coding system I use as an interlocutor, but it is not a sole authoritative voice on the requirements of preaching. However, it helped me understand nuances present in rhetorical coding and how the sermon genre has been discussed and considered within the field of rhetoric.

46 Donyelle McCray, "Quilting the Sermon: Homiletical Insights from Harriet Powers," *Religions* 9, no. 46 (2018): 1, https://doi.org/10.3390/rel9020046.

47 See also McClure, *Mashup Religion*, 2011.

48 McClure, *Speaking Together and with God*, xv.

49 McClure, *Speaking Together and with God*, xv.

50 McClure, *Speaking Together and with God*, 125.

51 McClure, *Speaking Together and with God*, 107.

52 Mountford, *Gendered Pulpit*, 13.

2 A Journey to Truth

1 Wendell Phillips said that Truth used to say this to him. Nell Irvin Painter, *Sojourner Truth: A Life, a Symbol* (New York: Norton, 1996), 255.

2 Sojourner Truth, "The Lord Has Made Me a Sign," in *Can I Get a Witness? Prophetic Religious Voices of African American Women: An Anthology*, ed. Marcia Y. Riggs (Maryknoll, NY: Orbis Books, 1997), 22.

3 The historical information that I have chosen to use is from Nell Irvin Painter's biography, *Sojourner Truth*, and Sojourner Truth's autobiography, *Narrative of Sojourner Truth* (Boston: 1850; repr., New York: Dover, 1997). While I read many other things, these two were most frequently referenced and gave the most comprehensive understanding of her life, offering critical details that shaped her homiletical prowess. Truth's autobiography talks about her life in vignettes and ends in the 1840s. Painter's biography then offers a robust secondary source to expand the story to the end of Truth's life and to fill in additional parts throughout.

4 Painter, *Sojourner Truth*, 114.

5 From this point on in this biographical sketch, I address Sojourner Truth as Isabella Baumfree, until the time in her life that she makes the choice to change her name to Sojourner Truth. This is the pattern that she follows in the *Narrative of Sojourner Truth*, and I aim to honor that pattern.

6 Truth, *Narrative of Sojourner Truth*, 5.

7 Truth, *Narrative of Sojourner Truth*, 7.

8 Truth, *Narrative of Sojourner Truth*, 10.

9 Painter, *Sojourner Truth*, 17.

10 Painter, *Sojourner Truth*, 16.

11 Truth, *Narrative of Sojourner Truth*, 14.

12 Painter, *Sojourner Truth*, 16.

13 Truth, *Narrative of Sojourner Truth*, 28.

14 Truth, *Narrative of Sojourner Truth*, 18.

15 Truth, *Narrative of Sojourner Truth*, 19.

16 The adoration of John Dumont is complicated and must be read within the context, violence, and specific particularities of narratives of those enslaved. There is a far more complicated and robust story than this brief outline. However, for the purposes of this book it is enough to know that she escaped from the Dumonts and encountered the Van Wagners, who took her in.

17 For more information on this religious organization, see Paul E. Johnson and Sean Wilentz, *The Kingdom of Matthias: A Story of Sex and Salvation in 19th-Century America* (New York: Oxford University Press, 2012).

18 Her preaching as Isabella Baumfree was different from her preaching as Sojourner Truth. Her later preaching in the context of freedom was not the same as preaching a particular evangelical agenda rooted in specific religious organizations, such as Perfectionism. I focus on her preaching as Truth. This time in her life, though, gave her experience preaching to mixed-race audiences, which may have served her as she considered the strategy for her preaching beyond the confines of this particular religious context.

19 Painter, *Sojourner Truth*, 51.

20 Painter, *Sojourner Truth*, 51.

21 Painter, *Sojourner Truth*, 53.

22 Painter, *Sojourner Truth*, 56.

23 Truth, *Narrative of Sojourner Truth*, 56.

24 Truth, *Narrative of Sojourner Truth*, 58. Truth is using "Spirit" to mean the Holy Spirit.

25 Painter, *Sojourner Truth*, 125–26.

26 Painter, *Sojourner Truth*, 126.

27 There isn't nearly as much detail around her other speeches as there is for the Women's Convention of 1851, primarily because of how famous her words at that conference (especially the rewritten words) have been throughout history. We have manuscripts for some speeches, but not as much information or even newspaper clippings describing them. I will be working from Robinson's account of Truth's words in the *Anti-Slavery Bugle* (June 21, 1851) rather than from those rewritten for publishing flair.

28 See Carleton Mabee and Susan Mabee Newhouse, *Sojourner Truth: Slave, Prophet, Legend* (New York: NYU Press, 1996).

29 As stated previously, I focused my attention on Truth's autobiography alongside Painter's biographical monograph. Other sources read but not referenced explicitly include: Carleton Mabee, "Sojourner Truth, Bold Prophet: Why Did She Never Learn to Read?" *New York History* 69, no. 1 (1988): 55–77, http://www.jstor.org/stable/23178487; Larry G. Murphy, *Sojourner Truth: A Biography* (Santa Barbara: Greenwood Biographies, 2011); Nell Irvin Painter, "Difference, Slavery, and Memory: Sojourner Truth in Feminist Abolitionism," in *The Abolitionist Sisterhood: Women's Political Culture in Antebellum America*, ed. Jean

Fagan Yellin and John C. Van Horne (Ithaca: Cornell University Press, 1994), 139–58, http://www.jstor.org/stable/10.7591/j.ctv1nhkdd.14; Nell Irvin Painter, "Representing Truth: Sojourner Truth's Knowing and Becoming Known," *Journal of American History* 81, no. 2 (1994): 461–92, https://doi.org/10.2307/2081168; Neil A. Patten, "The Nineteenth Century Black Woman as Social Reformer: The 'New' Speeches of Sojourner Truth," *Negro History Bulletin* 49, no. 1 (1986): 2–5, http://www.jstor.org/stable/44176646; Sallie M. Cuffee, "Reconstructing Subversive Moral Discourses in the Spiritual Autobiographies of Nineteenth-Century African American Preaching Women," *Journal of Feminist Studies in Religion* 32, no. 2 (2016): 45–62, https://doi.org/10.2979/jfemistudreli.32.2.05; Sojourner Truth, *Narrative of Sojourner Truth: A Northern Slave* (Boston: 1875), http://www.libraryweb.org/~digitized/books/Narrative_of_Sojourner_Truth.pdf.

30 Pulled and cross-referenced from Riggs, *Can I Get a Witness?* 22; Painter, *Sojourner Truth*, 125–26.

31 The legend often told is that Truth jumped up in a hostile white crowd to begin this particular speech, delivering it in a Southern dialect that (as a Northern, Dutch-speaking Black woman) she didn't even have. "Contrary to legend," Painter states, "Truth had not braved a hostile white crowd, for the crowd was friendly." Truth reported to a friend that she received more invitations to speak after the event in Akron, and, more importantly, she was able to sell many of her books that she had brought with her, which was her goal for more financial stability. Painter, *Sojourner Truth*, 129.

32 Pulled and cross-referenced from Sojourner Truth, "I Suppose I Am About the Only Colored Woman That Goes About to Speak for the Rights of Colored Women," in Riggs, *Can I Get a Witness?* 23; Sojourner Truth, "I Suppose I Am About the Only Colored Woman to Speak for the Rights of Colored Women—Sept. 7, 1853," speech given at the Fourth National Woman's Rights Convention in New York City, on September 7, 1853, https://awpc.cattcenter.iastate.edu/2017/03/21/suppose-i-am-about-the-only-colored-woman-to-speak-for-the-rights-of-colored-women-1853/.

33 Truth, *Narrative of Sojourner Truth*, 46.

34 In another artifact, "The Lord Has Made Me a Sign," Truth explicitly details her name change as having been given by God in this combination of "Sojourner" and "Truth." Continually speaking her name in spaces and standing as Sojourner Truth is the kind of re-signifying of freedom and agency that I assert here.

35 Truth, "Arn't I a Woman?" in Riggs, *Can I Get a Witness?* 21.

36 Truth, "Arn't I a Woman?" 21.

37 Truth, "I Suppose," 23.

38 Truth, "Arn't I a Woman?" 21.

39 Truth, "I Suppose," 23.

40 Truth, "I Suppose," 23.

41 In "Triple Consciousness: The Reimagination of Black Female Identities in Contemporary American Culture," Nahum Welang expands Du Bois's concept of double-consciousness that he posits in *Souls of Black Folk*, arguing that this is limited to Black men, and there is another layer for Black women. Welang writes, "Black women, due to the physical and psychological anguish they have historically endured on both fronts of race and gender, are fated to view themselves through three lenses and not two: *America* (represented by the hegemony of white patriarchy), *blackness* (a racial space that prioritizes the interests of black men) and *womanhood* (a hierarchical gendered identity with white women at the top and black women at the bottom)." Nahum Welang, "Triple Consciousness: The Reimagination of Black Female Identities in Contemporary American Culture," *Open Cultural Studies* 2, no. 1 (2018): 296–306, https://doi.org/10.1515/culture-2018-0027.

42 In *The Talking Book: African Americans and the Bible*, Allen Dwight Callahan offers a lens for understanding the Bible as it intersects with African American culture and how that intersection has historically created particular meanings and biblical themes for African American people. He writes, "African slaves and their descendants discerned something in the Bible that was neither at the center of their ancestral cultures nor in evidence in their hostile American home: a warrant for justice in this world." Allen Dwight Callahan, *The Talking Book: African Americans and the Bible* (New Haven: Yale University Press, 2006), xiv. In his chapter "The Talking Book," he talks about the ways that this written text lived in the hands of enslaved and previously enslaved people who were unable to read. African Americans took the Bible and created their own stories toward the aim of justice in this world for themselves. Truth uses her re-membering of Scripture as a practice toward justice through the abolitionist and women's rights movements.

43 Truth, "Arn't I a Woman?" 21–22.

44 Truth was known for her sarcasm as a part of her rhetorical strategies. Painter, *Sojourner Truth*, 127.

45 Truth, "Arn't I a Woman?" 22.

46 Truth, "Arn't I a Woman?" 22.

47 Truth, "Arn't I a Woman?" 22.

48 McClure, *Four Codes of Preaching*, 16–17.

49 Truth, "I Suppose," 23.

50 Sojourner Truth couldn't read or write, so she was rehearsing what she heard. Esther the individual is pulled out of the full context of the story, and Queen Vashti's narrative is not included, which would not have supported her point. However, her focus on normalizing Esther speaking to

the king allows her to normalize the idea that women should be free to speak to any authority.

51 Truth, "I Suppose," 23.
52 Truth, "I Suppose," 23.
53 See McClure, *Four Codes of Preaching*, 52–92.
54 See McClure, *Speaking Together and with God.*
55 Others assigned this name to Truth's work. I think it should be named "I Am a Woman's Rights."
56 Truth, "Arn't I a Woman?" 21.
57 Truth, "Arn't I a Woman?" 21–22.
58 Truth, "Arn't I a Woman?" 22.
59 Truth, "I Suppose," 23.
60 Truth, "I Suppose," 24.
61 Truth, "Arn't I a Woman?" 22.
62 McClure, *Four Codes of Preaching*, 41–42.
63 Thompson, *Ingenuity*, 175.
64 Truth, "I Suppose," 23.

3 A Commitment to Black Women, a Belief in Black People

1 Nannie Helen Burroughs, "The Path to Real Justice," in *Nannie Helen Burroughs: A Documentary Portrait of an Early Civil Rights Pioneer, 1900–1959*, ed. Kelisha B. Graves (Notre Dame: University of Notre Dame Press, 2019), 148; Nannie Helen Burroughs, "The Path to Real Justice," in *What Do You Think?* (Washington, DC, 1950), 105–11.
2 Susan Lindley, "'Neglected Voices' and Praxis in the Social Gospel," *Journal of Religious Ethics* 18, no. 1 (1990): 93.
3 Graves, *Nannie Helen Burroughs*, xv.
4 "As Burroughs's biographer and friend, Earl L. Harrison, recalled, 'like a tree she is better known by her fruit. She is so full of ideas and so imbued with the passion for service that she had no time to talk about Nannie.'" "Like many early twentieth century black women who were not only the inheritors of Victorian propriety but also the daughters of women whose claim to interiority was snatched away by slavery, Burroughs never willingly volunteered information about her private life or her past." Graves, *Nannie Helen Burroughs*, xxi.
5 Currently Virginia Union University, established in 1899.
6 Opal V. Easter, *Nannie Helen Burroughs* (New York: Garland, 1995), 27.
7 Graves, *Nannie Helen Burroughs*, xxii.
8 Graves, *Nannie Helen Burroughs*, xxii.
9 Nannie Helen Burroughs, "A Woman's Point of View," *Pittsburgh Courier*, September 17, 1930, 6, repr. in Graves, *Nannie Helen Burroughs*, 55–57.
10 Graves, *Nannie Helen Burroughs*, xxii.

11 Easter, *Nannie Helen Burroughs*, 17.

12 Burroughs didn't attend college. She received an honorary doctoral degree from Shaw University in 1944 when she was in her mid-sixties. Easter, *Nannie Helen Burroughs*, 26.

13 Easter, *Nannie Helen Burroughs*, 26, quoting Harrison, *Dream and the Dreamer*, in which he reprints a letter Burroughs wrote to Booker T. Washington requesting employment.

14 Easter, *Nannie Helen Burroughs*, 27.

15 This was the context of "How the Sisters Are Hindered from Helping."

16 Easter, *Nannie Helen Burroughs*, 29.

17 Easter, *Nannie Helen Burroughs*, 30.

18 Graves, *Nannie Helen Burroughs*, xxv.

19 Easter, *Nannie Helen Burroughs*, 31.

20 For example: "How: A Guide to the Missionary Society and Red Circle Guide for Christian Young People."

21 See Cheryl Townsend Gilkes, "'Sisters Who Can Lift Community': Nannie Helen Burroughs, 'The Slabtown District Convention,' and the Cultural Production of Community and Social Change," in Cheryl Townsend Gilkes, *"If It Wasn't for the Women . . .": Black Women's Experience and Womanist Culture in Church and Community* (Maryknoll, NY: Orbis Books, 2001), 142–57.

22 Easter, *Nannie Helen Burroughs*, 57, quoting Harrison, *Dream and the Dreamer*, 10.

23 Easter, *Nannie Helen Burroughs*, 58.

24 Easter, *Nannie Helen Burroughs*, 68.

25 Easter, *Nannie Helen Burroughs*, 82.

26 Evelyn Brooks Higginbotham, *Righteous Discontent: The Women's Movement in the Black Baptist Church, 1880–1920* (Cambridge, MA: Harvard University Press, 1993), 187.

27 Easter, *Nannie Helen Burroughs*, 63.

28 Easter, *Nannie Helen Burroughs*, 13.

29 Nannie Helen Burroughs to Mary Dorsett, May 12, 1956, Lincoln Heights, Washington, DC, http://www.nburroughsinfo.org/files/124835663.jpg.

30 Easter, *Nannie Helen Burroughs*, 64.

31 Easter, *Nannie Helen Burroughs*, 96–98.

32 Easter, *Nannie Helen Burroughs*, 105.

33 Graves, *Nannie Helen Burroughs*, xviii.

34 There were other moments that I could have examined that were even more explicitly wrapped in spiritual and religious thought, like "Reflections on Baptist Theology" or "The Role of Church and Society." However, I intentionally focused on works that are less explicitly about church or the Bible to note the ways that Burroughs is still using the same

rhetorical strategies in these different spheres and opening up opportunities for moral persuasion.

35 National Baptist Convention, *Journal of the Twentieth Annual Session for the National Baptist Convention, Held in Richmond, Virginia, September 12–17, 1900* (Nashville: National Baptist Publishing Board, 1900), 196–97, repr. as Nannie Helen Burroughs, "How the Sisters Are Hindered from Helping," in Graves, *Nannie Helen Burroughs*, 25–26.

36 Easter, *Nannie Helen Burroughs*, 27.

37 Irvine Garland Penn and John Wesley Edward Bowen, eds., *The United Negro, His Problems and His Progress: Containing the Address and Proceedings of the Negro Young People's Christian Congress, Held August 6–11, 1902* (Atlanta: D. E. Luther, 1902), 324–29, repr. as Nannie Helen Burroughs, "The Colored Woman and Her Relation to the Domestic Problem," in Graves, *Nannie Helen Burroughs*, 27–31.

38 "Negro Young People's Christian and Educational Congress, Atlanta, Ga., Aug. 6–12, 1902," in *Newspaper Clipping, Logbooks, Journals & Scrapbooks* 12 (2018), 19, http://dh.howard.edu/og_news/12.

39 Another clip said, "The following address by Nannie H. Burroughs of Washington D.C., on 'The Colored Woman and her Relation to the Domestic Problem,' probably created a stronger impression than any address heard at the negro congress." "Negro Young People's Christian and Educational Congress," 26.

40 Graves, *Nannie Helen Burroughs*, xxxiv.

41 Burroughs, "How the Sisters," 26.

42 Burroughs, "The Domestic Problem," 27.

43 Some reiterations of this sentiment include: "The solution of this problem will be the prime factor in the salvation of Negro womanhood, whose salvation must be attained before the so-called race problem can be solved." "The subject of domestic science has crowded itself upon us, and unless we receive it, master it and be wise, the next ten years will so revolutionize things that we will find our women without the wherewith to support themselves." "What will this crowding from service mean to Negro women? It will mean their degradation." Burroughs, "The Domestic Problem," 27–31.

44 Burroughs, "How the Sisters," 26.

45 Certainly, our notions of missiology have changed, and this language would not be appropriate now. However, we must root Burroughs in her context. It would be far easier to critique someone today for saying this, but to critique out of context doesn't actually help us in understanding her rhetoric.

46 Burroughs, "How the Sisters," 26.

47 Burroughs, "How the Sisters," 26.

48 Burroughs, "How the Sisters," 25–26.

49 "Negro Young People's Christian and Educational Congress," 26.

50 Burroughs, “How the Sisters,” 25.
51 Burroughs, “How the Sisters,” 26.
52 Burroughs, “The Domestic Problem,” 29.
53 Burroughs, “The Domestic Problem,” 28.
54 Burroughs, “The Domestic Problem,” 28–29.
55 Burroughs, “How the Sisters,” 26.
56 Burroughs, “How the Sisters,” 26.
57 Burroughs, “The Domestic Problem,” 29.
58 Burroughs, “The Domestic Problem,” 30.
59 Burroughs, “The Domestic Problem,” 29.
60 Burroughs, “The Domestic Problem,” 29.

4 Too Sick to Be Silent, Too Tired Not to Talk

1 Fannie Lou Hamer, “‘I'm Sick and Tired of Being Sick and Tired,’ Speech Delivered with Malcolm X at the Williams Institutional CME Church, Harlem, New York, December 20, 1964,” in *Speeches of Fannie Lou Hamer: To Tell It Like It Is*, ed. Maegan Parker Brooks and Davis W. Houck (Jackson: University Press of Mississippi, 2010), 75–80.
2 Fannie Lou Hamer, *To Praise Our Bridges: An Autobiography of Mrs. Fanny Lou Hamer*, ed. Julius Lester (Washington, DC: KIPCO, 1967), 17; Fannie Lou Hamer, “To Praise Our Bridges,” in *Mississippi Writers: Reflections of Childhood and Youth*, vol. 2, ed. Dorothy Abbott (Jackson: University Press of Mississippi, 1986), 324, https://snccdigital.org/wp-content/themes/sncc/flipbooks/mev_hamer_updated_2018/index.html?swipeboxvideo=1#page/6.
3 Reminiscing on a white mob, Hamer said: “I ain't never heard of no one white man going to get a Negro. They're the most cowardly people I know.” Kay Mills, *This Little Light of Mine: The Life of Fannie Lou Hamer* (New York: Penguin Books, 1993), 11.
4 Chana Kai Lee, *For Freedom's Sake: The Life of Fannie Lou Hamer* (Chicago: University of Illinois Press, 1999), 1.
5 Hamer, *To Praise Our Bridges*, 11; Hamer, “To Praise Our Bridges,” 324.
6 Interview with Fannie Lou Hamer, *The Independent Eye* (Cincinnati, OH), December 23, 1968–January 20, 1969.
7 Hamer, *To Praise Our Bridges*, 11.
8 Hamer, *To Praise Our Bridges*, 9.
9 Hamer, *To Praise Our Bridges*, 11.
10 Lee, *For Freedom's Sake*, 14–15.
11 Lee, *For Freedom's Sake*, 5.
12 Maegan Parker Brooks, *A Voice That Could Stir an Army: Fannie Lou Hamer and the Rhetoric of the Black Freedom Movement* (Jackson: University Press of Mississippi, 2014), 19–20.
13 Mills, *This Little Light of Mine*, 12.

14 Susan Kling, *Fannie Lou Hamer: A Biography* (New York: Women for Racial and Economic Equality, 1979), 12.
15 Mills, *This Little Light of Mine*, 18.
16 Lee, *For Freedom's Sake*, 21.
17 Mills, *This Little Light of Mine*, 21.
18 Hamer, *To Praise Our Bridges*, 12.
19 Lee, *For Freedom's Sake*, 25; June Jordan, *Fannie Lou Hamer* (New York: Crowell, 1972), 24.
20 Lee, *For Freedom's Sake*, x.
21 Lee, *For Freedom's Sake*, 30.
22 Hamer, *To Praise Our Bridges*, 20.
23 Lee, *For Freedom's Sake*, 34.
24 Lee, *For Freedom's Sake*, 51.
25 Earnest N. Bracey, *Fannie Lou Hamer: The Life of a Civil Rights Icon* (Jefferson, NC: McFarland, 2011), 87.
26 Hamer, *To Praise Our Bridges*, 14.
27 Lee, *For Freedom's Sake*, 55.
28 Lee, *For Freedom's Sake*, 57.
29 Lee, *For Freedom's Sake*, 58.
30 Lee, *For Freedom's Sake*, 58.
31 Lee, *For Freedom's Sake*, 98–99.
32 Lee, *For Freedom's Sake*, x.
33 Quoted in Mills, *This Little Light of Mine*, 19.
34 Bracey, *Fannie Lou Hamer*, 3.
35 Fannie Lou Hamer, "'We're on Our Way,' Speech Delivered at a Mass Meeting in Indianola, Mississippi, September 1964," in Brooks and Houck, *Speeches of Fannie Lou Hamer*, 66.
36 To recount every piece of testimony in this artifact would be to rehearse the entire artifact in a way that would not be productive; however, I aim to offer clear examples so that readers can see how testimony is operative and how it becomes the foundation for the other homiletical insights. Hamer, "We're on Our Way," 66.
37 Hamer, "We're on Our Way," 66–67.
38 Hamer, "We're on Our Way," 67.
39 Hamer, "We're on Our Way," 67.
40 Hamer, "We're on Our Way," 67.
41 Hamer, "We're on Our Way," 67.
42 Hamer, "We're on Our Way," 67.
43 Hamer, "We're on Our Way," 67.
44 This is a sampling of the testimony in the sermon. It is a forty-five-minute sermon that includes several minutes of detailed testimony. Hamer also recounts in detail the events of Winona. Similar to this series of testimony, she follows up with a question about the state of affairs. She then says, "But I want the people to know in Mississippi today, the cover

has been pulled back off of you and you don't have any place to hide." Hamer, "We're on Our Way," 66–74.

45 Fannie Lou Hamer, "'We Haven't Arrived Yet,' Presentation and Responses to Questions at the University of Wisconsin, Madison, Wisconsin, January 29, 1976," in Brooks and Houck, *Speeches of Fannie Lou Hamer*, 179.
46 Hamer, "We Haven't Arrived Yet," 177.
47 Hamer, "We Haven't Arrived Yet," 177.
48 Hamer, "We're on Our Way," 72 (emphasis added).
49 Hamer, "We're on Our Way," 72 (emphasis added).
50 Hamer, "We're on Our Way," 73 (emphasis added).
51 Hamer, "We Haven't Arrived Yet," 178.
52 Hamer, "We're on Our Way," 68.
53 Hamer, "We're on Our Way," 68.
54 Hamer, "We Haven't Arrived Yet," 177.
55 Hamer, "We Haven't Arrived Yet," 179.
56 Hamer, "We're on Our Way," 68.
57 Hamer, "We're on Our Way," 68.
58 Hamer, "We're on Our Way," 68.
59 Hamer, "We're on Our Way," 69.
60 Hamer, "We're on Our Way," 73.
61 Hamer, "We're on Our Way," 68.
62 Hamer, "We're on Our Way," 71.
63 Hamer, "We're on Our Way," 71.
64 Such comments included: "As an orator, Hamer was extraordinary—a black heroine who gave 'hair raising' speeches against the Mississippi political establishment all over the country." Mills, *This Little Light of Mine*, 9.
65 Hamer, *To Praise Our Bridges*, 16.

5 Conclusion

1 I want to be clear that I am not discounting pulpit preaching as an important practice. I assert that pulpit preaching is one form of preaching, not preaching in its entirety, and that studying preachers beyond the limitations of this space offers us a robustness to the understanding of preaching, including who can do it and which proclaimers are a part of our historical preaching lineage.
2 Florence, *Preaching as Testimony*, xxvi–xxvii.
3 Thompson, *Ingenuity*, 107.

BIBLIOGRAPHY

Allen, Donna E. *Toward a Womanist Homiletic: Katie Cannon, Alice Walker and Emancipatory Proclamation*. New York: Lang, 2013.

Bitzer, Lloyd F. "The Rhetorical Situation." *Philosophy & Rhetoric* 1, no. 1 (1968): 1–14. https://www.jstor.org/stable/40236733.

Bivins, Jason C. *Religion of Fear: The Politics of Horror in Conservative Evangelicalism*. New York: Oxford University Press, 2008.

Bracey, Earnest N. *Fannie Lou Hamer: The Life of a Civil Rights Icon*. Jefferson, NC: McFarland, 2011.

Brooks, Maegan Parker. *A Voice That Could Stir an Army: Fannie Lou Hamer and the Rhetoric of the Black Freedom Movement*. Jackson: University Press of Mississippi, 2014.

Brown, Teresa L. Fry. *Weary Throats and New Songs: Black Women Proclaiming God's Word*. Nashville: Abingdon, 2003.

Burroughs, Nannie Helen. "The Colored Woman and Her Relation to the Domestic Problem." In *Nannie Helen Burroughs: A Documentary Portrait of an Early Civil Rights Pioneer, 1900–1959*, edited and annotated by Kelisha B. Graves, 27–31. Notre Dame: University of Notre Dame Press, 2019.

Burroughs, Nannie Helen. "How the Sisters Are Hindered from Helping." In *Nannie Helen Burroughs: A Documentary Portrait of an Early Civil Rights Pioneer, 1900–1959*, edited and annotated by Kelisha B. Graves, 25–26. Notre Dame: University of Notre Dame Press, 2019.

Burroughs, Nannie Helen. Letter to Mary Dorsett, May 12, 1956, Lincoln Heights, Washington, DC. http://www.nburroughsinfo.org/files/124835663.jpg.

Burroughs, Nannie Helen. "The Path to Real Justice." In *What Do You Think?* 105–11. Washington, DC, 1950. Included in *Nannie Helen Burroughs: A Documentary Portrait of an Early Civil Rights Pioneer, 1900–1959*, edited and annotated by Kelisha B. Graves, 148. Notre Dame: University of Notre Dame Press, 2019.

Burroughs, Nannie Helen. "A Woman's Point of View." *Pittsburgh Courier*, September 17, 1930.

Callahan, Allen Dwight. *The Talking Book: African Americans and the Bible*. New Haven: Yale University Press, 2006.

Cannon, Katie G. *Katie's Canon: Womanism and the Soul of the Black Community*. New York: Continuum, 1995.

Carvalhaes, Cláudio. "Forms of Speech, Religion, and Social Resistance." *CrossCurrents* 66, no. 2 (2016): 136–53. https://doi.org/10.1111/cros.12183.

Collins, Patricia Hill, and Sirma Bilge. *Intersectionality*. Cambridge: Polity, 2016.

Crenshaw, Kimberle. "Mapping the Margins: Intersectionality, Identity Politics, and Violence Against Women of Color." *Stanford Law Review* 43, no. 6 (1991): 1241–99. https://www.jstor.org/stable/1229039.

Cuffee, Sallie M. "Reconstructing Subversive Moral Discourses in the Spiritual Autobiographies of Nineteenth-Century African American Preaching Women." *Journal of Feminist Studies in Religion* 32, no. 2 (2016): 45–62. https://doi.org/10.2979/jfemistudreli.32.2.05.

Easter, Opal V. *Nannie Helen Burroughs*. New York: Garland, 1995.

Florence, Anna Carter. *Preaching as Testimony*. Louisville: Westminster John Knox, 2007.

Floyd-Thomas, Stacey M., ed. *Deeper Shades of Purple: Womanism in Religion and Society*. Minneapolis: Graywolf, 2016.

Gilbert, Kenyatta R. *The Journey and Promise of African American Preaching*. Minneapolis: Fortress, 2011.

Gilkes, Cheryl Townsend. *"If It Wasn't for the Women . . .": Black Women's Experience and Womanist Culture in Church and Community*. Maryknoll, NY: Orbis Books, 2001.

Graves, Kelisha B., ed. *Nannie Helen Burroughs: A Documentary Portrait of an Early Civil Rights Pioneer, 1900–1959*. Notre Dame: University of Notre Dame Press, 2019.

Hamer, Fannie Lou. "'I'm Sick and Tired of Being Sick and Tired,' Speech Delivered with Malcolm X at the Williams Institutional CME Church, Harlem, New York, December 20, 1964." In *Speeches of Fannie Lou Hamer: To Tell It Like It Is*, edited by Maegan

Parker Brooks and Davis W. Houck, 75–80. Jackson: University Press of Mississippi, 2010.

Hamer, Fannie Lou. *To Praise Our Bridges: An Autobiography of Mrs. Fanny Lou Hamer*. Edited by Julius Lester. Washington, DC: KIPCO, 1967.

Hamer, Fannie Lou. "To Praise Our Bridges." In *Mississippi Writers: Reflections of Childhood and Youth*, vol. 2, edited by Dorothy Abbott, 324. Jackson: University Press of Mississippi, 1986. https://snccdigital.org/wp-content/themes/sncc/flipbooks/mev_hamer_updated_2018/index.html?swipeboxvideo=1#page/6.

Hamer, Fannie Lou. "'We Haven't Arrived Yet,' Presentation and Responses to Questions at the University of Wisconsin, Madison, Wisconsin, January 29, 1976." In *Speeches of Fannie Lou Hamer: To Tell It Like It Is*, edited by Maegan Parker Brooks and Davis W. Houck, 176–85. Jackson: University Press of Mississippi, 2010.

Hamer, Fannie Lou. "'We're on Our Way,' Speech Delivered at a Mass Meeting in Indianola, Mississippi, September 1964." In *Speeches of Fannie Lou Hamer: To Tell It Like It Is*, edited by Maegan Parker Brooks and Davis W. Houck, 66–74. Jackson: University Press of Mississippi, 2010.

Higginbotham, Evelyn Brooks. *Righteous Discontent: The Women's Movement in the Black Baptist Church, 1880–1920*. Cambridge, MA: Harvard University Press, 1993.

Interview with Fannie Lou Hamer, *The Independent Eye* (Cincinnati, OH), December 23, 1968–January 20, 1969.

Johnson, Kimberly. *The Womanist Preacher: Reclaiming Womanist Rhetoric from the Pulpit*. Lanham: Lexington Books, 2017.

Johnson, Paul E., and Sean Wilentz. *The Kingdom of Matthias: A Story of Sex and Salvation in 19th-Century America*. New York: Oxford University Press, 2012.

Jordan, June. *Fannie Lou Hamer*. New York: Crowell, 1972.

Kilde, Jeanne Halgren. *Sacred Power, Sacred Space: An Introduction to Christian Architecture and Worship*. New York: Oxford University Press, 2008.

Kling, Susan. *Fannie Lou Hamer: A Biography*. New York: Women for Racial and Economic Equality, 1979.

LaRue, Cleophus J. *The Heart of Black Preaching*. Louisville: Westminster John Knox, 2000.

Lee, Chana Kai. *For Freedom's Sake: The Life of Fannie Lou Hamer*. Chicago: University of Illinois Press, 1999.

Lindley, Susan. "'Neglected Voices' and Praxis in the Social Gospel." *Journal of Religious Ethics* 18, no. 1 (1990): 93.

Long, Thomas G. *The Witness of Preaching*. Louisville: Westminster John Knox, 2005.

Lundberg, Christian. *Lacan in Public: Psychoanalysis and the Science of Rhetoric*. Tuscaloosa: University of Alabama Press, 2012.

Mabee, Carleton. "Sojourner Truth, Bold Prophet: Why Did She Never Learn to Read?" *New York History* 69, no. 1 (1988): 55–77. http://www.jstor.org/stable/23178487.

Mabee, Carleton, and Susan Mabee Newhouse. *Sojourner Truth: Slave, Prophet, Legend*. New York: NYU Press, 1995.

McClure, John S. *The Four Codes of Preaching: Rhetorical Strategies*. Louisville: Westminster John Knox, 2003.

McClure, John S. *Mashup Religion: Pop Music and Theological Invention*. Waco, TX: Baylor University Press, 2011.

McClure, John S. *The Roundtable Pulpit: Where Leadership and Preaching Meet*. Nashville: Abingdon, 1995.

McClure, John S. *Speaking Together and with God: Liturgy and Communicative Ethics*. Lanham, MD: Lexington Books, 2018.

McCormack, Michael Brandon. "'What in God's Name Is the Point?!': Theorizing Ritual, Representation and Resistance in African American Religious Thought and Practice." *Practical Matters* 8 (March 2015): 16–36. http://practicalmattersjournal.org/2015/03/01/what-in-gods-name.

McCray, Donyelle C. *The Censored Pulpit: Julian of Norwich as Preacher*. London: Lexington Books, 2019.

McCray, Donyelle. "Quilting the Sermon: Homiletical Insights from Harriet Powers." *Religions* 9, no. 46 (2018): 1–7. https://doi.org/10.3390/rel9020046.

Mills, Kay. *This Little Light of Mine: The Life of Fannie Lou Hamer*. New York: Penguin Books, 1993.

Mitchell, Henry H. *Black Preaching: The Recovery of a Powerful Art*. Nashville: Abingdon, 1990.

Mountford, Roxanne. *The Gendered Pulpit: Preaching in American Protestant Spaces*. Carbondale: Southern Illinois University Press, 2005.

Murphy, Larry G. *Sojourner Truth: A Biography*. Santa Barbara: Greenwood Biographies, 2011.

National Baptist Convention. *Journal of the Twentieth Annual Session for the National Baptist Convention, Held in Richmond, Virginia, September 12–17, 1900*. Nashville: National Baptist Publishing Board, 1900.

"Negro Young People's Christian and Educational Congress, Atlanta, Ga., Aug. 6–12, 1902." In *Newspaper Clipping, Logbooks, Journals & Scrapbooks* 12 (2018). http://dh.howard.edu/og_news/12.

Otis, Hailey Nicole. "Intersectional Rhetoric: Where Intersectionality as Analytic Sensibility and Embodied Rhetorical Praxis Converge." *Quarterly Journal of Speech* 105, no. 4 (2019): 369–89. https://doi.org/10.1080/00335630.2019.1664755.

Painter, Nell Irvin. "Difference, Slavery, and Memory: Sojourner Truth in Feminist Abolitionism." In *The Abolitionist Sisterhood: Women's Political Culture in Antebellum America*, edited by Jean Fagan Yellin and John C. Van Horne, 139–58. Ithaca: Cornell University Press, 1994. http://www.jstor.org/stable/10.7591/j.ctv1nhkdd.14.

Painter, Nell Irvin. "Representing Truth: Sojourner Truth's Knowing and Becoming Known." *Journal of American History* 81, no. 2 (1994): 461–92. https://doi.org/10.2307/2081168.

Painter, Nell Irvin. *Sojourner Truth: A Life, a Symbol.* New York: Norton, 1996.

Patten, Neil A. "The Nineteenth Century Black Woman as Social Reformer: The 'New' Speeches of Sojourner Truth." *Negro History Bulletin* 49, no. 1 (1986): 2–5. http://www.jstor.org/stable/44176646.

Penn, Irvine Garland, and John Wesley Edward Bowen, eds. *The United Negro, His Problems and His Progress: Containing the Address and Proceedings of the Negro Young People's Christian Congress, Held August 6–11, 1902*. Atlanta: D. E. Luther, 1902.

Powery, Luke A. *Spirit Speech*. Nashville: Abingdon, 2009.

Riggs, Marcia Y., ed. *Can I Get a Witness? Prophetic Religious Voices of African American Women: An Anthology*. Maryknoll, NY: Orbis Books, 1997.

Rose, Lucy Atkinson. *Sharing the Word: Preaching in the Roundtable Church*. Louisville: Westminster John Knox, 1997.

Smith, Christine M. *Weaving the Sermon: Preaching in a Feminist Perspective*. Louisville: Westminster John Knox, 1989.

Thomas, Frank. *How to Preach a Dangerous Sermon*. Nashville: Abingdon, 2018.

Thomas, Frank. *They Like to Never Quit Praisin' God: The Role of Celebration in Preaching*. Rev. ed. Cleveland: Pilgrim, 2013.

Thompson, Lisa L. *Ingenuity: Preaching as an Outsider*. Nashville: Abingdon, 2018.

Townes, Emilie M. "Womanist Theology." *Union Seminary Quarterly Review* 57, no. 3 (2003): 159–76.

Truth, Sojourner. "Arn't I a Woman?" In *Can I Get a Witness? Prophetic Religious Voices of African American Women: An Anthology*, edited by Marcia Y. Riggs, 21–22. Maryknoll, NY: Orbis Books, 1997.

Truth, Sojourner. "I Suppose I Am About the Only Colored Woman That Goes About to Speak for the Rights of Colored Women." In *Can I Get a Witness? Prophetic Religious Voices of African American Women: An Anthology*, edited by Marcia Y. Riggs, 23–24. Maryknoll, NY: Orbis Books, 1997.

Truth, Sojourner. "I Suppose I Am About the Only Colored Woman to Speak for the Rights of Colored Women—Sept. 7, 1853." Speech given at the Fourth National Woman's Rights Convention in New York City, on September 7, 1853. https://awpc.cattcenter.iastate.edu/2017/03/21/suppose-i-am-about-the-only-colored-woman-to-speak-for-the-rights-of-colored-women-1853/.

Truth, Sojourner. "The Lord Has Made Me a Sign." In *Can I Get a Witness? Prophetic Religious Voices of African American Women: An Anthology*, edited by Marcia Y. Riggs, 22. Maryknoll, NY: Orbis Books, 1997.

Truth, Sojourner. *Narrative of Sojourner Truth*. New York: Dover, 1997.

Turner, Mary Donovan, and Mary Lin Hudson. *Saved from Silence: Finding Women's Voice in Preaching*. St. Louis: Lucas Park Books, 2014.

Welang, Nahum. "Triple Consciousness: The Reimagination of Black Female Identities in Contemporary American Culture." *Open Cultural Studies* 2, no. 1 (2018): 96–306. https://doi.org/10.1515/culture-2018-0027.

Zink-Sawyer, Beverly. *From Preachers to Suffragists: Woman's Rights and Religious Conviction in the Lives of Three Nineteenth-Century American Clergywomen*. Louisville: Westminster John Knox, 2003.

INDEX